Praise for WORST LAID PLANS

"I admit to being attracted to most of the women in this book, so reading it was an embarrassing sexual experience in itself. This is the best kind of comedy; that which makes you both laugh and erect."

—**Rob Corddry** (*The Daily Show*)

"*Worst Laid Plans* is irrefutable evidence that one should wait until marriage to have sex."

—**Joel McHale** (*The Soup*, *Community*)

"This collection of stories will make you scream, blush, wince, cringe, gag, and laugh out loud. Mainly, reading this book will make you feel thankful. Thankful these brave foot soldiers entered battle and lived to tell about it. All you have to do is curl up with a bottle of pinot grigio and a bag of mint milanos and settle in for an evening you won't have to regret later."

—**Casey Wilson** (*SNL*, *Bride Wars*)

"They say that 'truth is comedy,' and it can't get any truthier than people telling stories about bad sex."

—**Matt Besser** (founding member of the Upright Citizens Brigade)

"Hilarious. This is the kind of book you don't take home to meet the parents."

—**Teri Polo** (*Meet the Parents*, *Meet the Fockers, Little Fockers*)

"Good book. Good dames."

—**Tony Sirico** (*The Sopranos*)

"These outrageous stories are both hilarious and full of truth. What was great onstage is an even better read from the privacy of your own home!"

—**Alison Brie** (*Community*, *Mad Men*)

"This book boldly goes where no book has ever gone before. You know what? It goes boldly where no porn has ever gone before. Where this book goes Tommy Lee hasn't even gone! It will make you laugh, it will make you cry (if you're as emotionally unstable as I am) and it will make you worried about the psychical and mental health of us *Worst Laid Plans*-ers."

—**Whitney Cummings** (*Chelsea Lately*)

Based on the comedy show performed at
the **Upright Citizens Brigade Theatre**

WORST LAID PLANS

When Bad Sex Happens
to Good People

True Tales Edited by
Alexandra Lydon and **Laura Kindred**

ABRAMS IMAGE, NEW YORK

In the interest of maintaining the privacy of the individuals whose stories
are dicussed herein, many names, places, and other identifying characteristics
have been changed.

Based on the stage show created by Alexandra Lydon and Laura Kindred

ISBN 978-0-8109-8902-3

Library of Congress Cataloging-in-Publication Data

Worst laid plans : when bad sex happens to good people : true tales / edited
by Alexandra Lydon and Laura Kindred.
   p. cm.
 ISBN 978-0-8109-8902-3
 1. Sex—Humor. 2. Sex—Miscellanea. I. Lydon, Alexandra. II. Kindred,
Laura.
 HQ25.W67 2010
 306.77—dc22

                            2009046123

Printed and bound in U.S.A.
10 9 8 7 6 5 4 3 2 1

Abrams Image books are available at special discounts when purchased in
quantity for premiums and promotions as well as fundraising or educational
use. Special editions can also be created to specification. For details, contact
specialmarkets@abramsbooks.com, or the address below.

ABRAMS IM▲GE

An imprint of ABRAMS
115 West 18th Street
New York, NY 10011
www.abramsbooks.com

The following stories are based on true events. Some names and key details have been changed to protect the guilty.

Except for Raymond.

This one's for you ... wherever you are.

TABLE OF EXPLICIT CONTENT:

*When bad sex happens to good people,
there's no recourse like full disclosure.*

ABOUT THE STAGE SHOW

Worst Laid Plans premiered at the Upright Citizens Brigade Theatre in Los Angeles in July 2007. It was conceived by Laura Kindred and Alexandra Lydon following a particularly noteworthy coital catastrophe on foreign soil. For the full story, please skip ahead to "The Farting Rapist." The next morning, while regrouping and attempting to regain lost dignity, these two friends discovered bad sex's greatest palliative: disclosure.

After sharing this hard-won revelation, they gathered a dream team of performers to create the stage show *Worst Laid Plans: True Stories of Terrible Sex*. And like a venereal disease, the word spread, creating a surge of graphic co-misery. The show continues to run at the Upright Citizens Brigade Theatre in Los Angeles and New York City, and has welcomed such celebrity comediennes as Janeane Garofalo, Amy Poehler, Mary Lynn Rajskub, Laraine Newman, and many more.

Having enjoyed such success in the oral tradition, it has come time for these sexual tragedies to be immortalized in print.

FOREWORD by Laraine Newman

All roads lead to sex. It's the reason we strive. Strive for excellence, piety, beauty, discovery, invention, and conquest.

Don't kid yourself. Do you really think Leonard Susskind, known as the father of string theory, pursued theoretical physics and quantum mechanics in order to satisfy his need for symmetry in the universe? Fuck no. It was for the chicks!

Sex is the motivator. It inspires us to greatness.

Regrettably as you will see in this book, it also takes people of great sensitivity and otherwise inherent dignity and puts a filthy boot on their necks.

In these pages, you will be privy to the experiences of the brave soldiers who have fallen on the swords of sexual folly and its many nasty cousins—so wide-ranging and wondrous, you can bet a pimpled porn star's ass there's something here for everyone.

What's ironic is that it takes considerable objectivity and a, you should excuse the expression (since this condition is so often absent in these escapades), "sober eye," to be able to bring these stories to you with such honesty, wit, and perspective.

After seeing the stage show and laughing so hard my lungs hurt, I felt a sense of longing. Is this it? I thought, I want more.

So, here, people, are the keys to the kingdom.

Worst Laid Plans is a hilarious testimonial to the vast array of consequences we face after having ignored that little voice inside that says: "Don't." "This isn't a good idea." "Leave now."

INTRODUCTION

Alex and Laura here. Your editors.

Like the kid who kicked you in the crotch in third grade, we'd like to start by saying:

You're welcome.

We've all been there. We've all had that moment. You look back and remember when you made that crucial decision and realize why: You just got dumped; you had eight whiskeys; sure, she's batshit insane, but she's *also* a model. You had your reasons. And then the aftermath. You take in your surroundings and see his sheets are printed with cartoon characters. You sober up with two sets of hands in your nethers and remember you have a boyfriend. Yes, your pap smear is, and now forever will be, "abnormal." You're fucked—figuratively and literally.

But you're not alone.

What connects us as human beings are the fundamental needs we all share: to be seen, to be loved, to not have ejaculate thrown in our faces. To be understood. In our quest to find these things we can run up against the unexpected obstacle or the occasional setback: low self-esteem, extreme intoxication, Craigslist.

And that's okay. If this book has any message, any wisdom to dispense at all, it's just that:

It's okay.

So let's hold hands—it doesn't have to go any further than that—and go through this together.

Open your mind, open your heart, turn the page, and just relax, baby. Unlike the high school quarterback when he promised you were gonna like it, we're telling the truth.

CHAPTER 1

THE END OF INNOCENCE

a memorial to virginity

Virginity. What can we say about virginity? It was a good friend; it was with us from day one. We knew we wouldn't have it forever, but we weren't ready to say good-bye. We went everywhere together: camp, classes, weddings, church, bat mitzvahs. It was pure. It was clean. It was innocent. Sure, it could be a little uptight, and yes, there were times when we'd pretend we didn't know it because it wasn't "cool." But to have it taken from us so suddenly? To lose it like that?

And at the prom no less.

CONFESSIONS OF A TEENAGE MIME

by Amy Rhodes

In high school I was a mime.

Also, I was a virgin.

These two things were directly related, although I didn't realize it at the time.

As I sat in front of a mirror, carefully applying my white cake makeup, putting on my white gloves, and adjusting my bow tie, it never occurred to me to stop and say, "This right here, Amy? This is the reason that no guy is sticking his dick in you."

It's not like I didn't think about sex in high school. Every day for four years I thought about what it would be like to have sex with Kevin Jacobson. I imagined us having sex in a hot tub, because Sarah Shirk told me that that's where she lost her virginity to Brad Griffith when his parents went to see the Iowa Hawkeyes play in the Rose Bowl.

But I also thought about how perfect it would be to use the George Michael song "Mother's Pride" in a sketch the mime troupe was working on about a young soldier. And I thought about how, at the end of the sketch, when the soldier's widowed wife watches her son go off to fight in the same war his father died in, it would blow people's minds.

And the thing is, when you think about stuff like that, no matter how much you also think about sex, you're not going to get laid.

When I went to college, I put a framed picture of my

mime troupe on my dorm room desk. But college was new and exciting, and I quickly forgot it was even there. That is, until the night a guy from Tilton Hall came over to hang out, saw it, and asked, "What the hell is this? Were you a clown or something?"

"Please. Like I would be a clown," I scoffed. "I was a mime."

He just stared at me. I stared back. Then he kissed me. I'd been kissed before, but this was different. And when he took off his shirt and pants, I knew there was more to come. So I panicked.

In an attempt to lighten the mood, I pulled out an old routine. For my high school mime troupe audition, I did a sketch where I was in a Laundromat when I realized that the clothes I was wearing were dirty and, forgetting I was in public, took them off and put them in the washer with the rest of my laundry. Now, standing in front of the guy from Tilton Hall, I started pretending to unbutton the top button of my blouse, then the next and the next, shimmying out of it as it fell to the floor. Even though I was still fully clothed, I felt totally naked miming without my white makeup on, so I stopped before I got to my pants.

"It's better with the music," I said. "That song 'Dirty Laundry' by Don Henley. It's better as a full performance piece. . . ."

He just stared at me. I stared back. Then he kissed me again as he *actually* took off my shirt and pants. And, because I had both the top bunk and a blatant disregard for other people's personal space, we had sex on my roommate's bed.

As soon as we started I realized I had no idea how to

behave. For the four years I'd been a mime, no guy had come anywhere near my vagina. While other girls were giving blowjobs, getting fingerblasted,* and screwing guys in hot tubs, I was leaning against invisible walls, getting trapped in make-believe boxes, and acting like I was running into the wind. Now some guy was not just near my vagina; he was inside of it.

Lying on my roommate's bed and losing my virginity, I thought about how, as a mime, I'd been able to express the terror of riding a roller coaster, the frustration of getting gum stuck to the bottom of my shoe, and the joy of opening a small box to find an engagement ring inside without ever uttering a single word. But I knew if I wanted to express myself now, I could no longer be silent. If I wanted this guy to know I liked having sex, I needed my voice to be heard.

So, I decided it was time to be loud. Really loud. I yelled, "Yes!" and screamed, "Don't stop!" and scream-yelled, "Yes, don't stop!" as loud as I could. I imagined that my voice was carrying all the way to Houston Hall. I envisioned people gathering in the dining hall, saying, "I can hear someone in Hill Hall having sex, and that's across the quad. Wow. That person is loud."

It was as though the guy from Tilton Hall was fucking the mime right out of me.

Then, suddenly, he was done. After a few minutes he got up, put on his clothes, and said he had to go meet someone in the computer lab.

---

* For definitions of terms marked with an asterisk please refer to the glossary.

When I saw him in the cafeteria the next morning, he pretended like nothing had happened. Maybe it had been really obvious that I didn't know what I was doing. Maybe he doesn't like screamers. Maybe he was embarrassed that, as I'd find out with more experience, he had a small dick and had come too quickly. Or maybe he was just an asshole. With time I've come to realize it doesn't really matter.

At the end of my final Spring-Night-O-Mime show at the end of high school, I, like the other graduating mimes, had walked to the center of the stage, stood in a pool of light, and taken off my white bow tie and gloves. In just a black leotard and tights, I exited the theatre through the audience. I had technically left the mime behind that day, but I didn't really find my voice until I heard it yelling, "Yes! Don't stop!"

And it didn't.

Marcel Marceau once said, "Never get a mime talking. He won't stop." It's true.

THE VIRGIN QUEEN

by Waitress, NYC, 30

Growing up, I was freakishly small and no one paid attention to me. There are always a few—those gnomes of the schoolyard running in slow motion toward puberty. But we sad sideshows were the same as our peers emotionally, if not physically. In junior high, I shaved my legs and wore a training bra, which, by the way, was too big in the smallest size. I always wore a T-shirt if there was going to be any swimming, until one pool party when Ben DeCroce convinced me to doff my cover-up only to respond in disbelief, "Wow, you really *are* flat!" And even though there's no audience of cruel eighth graders (whatever, Ben, like you were some prize with your gross glasses and chinlessness) to stare in appalled silence at this story and all its shirtless flatness, the spirit is the same. Take *that*, Holly McKinley, who was fully boobed and pubed by age thirteen and getting it on with a twenty-two-year-old. I may not have gotten to second base until I was eighteen, but at least *I* didn't get molested.

This is actually a sore spot for me. By sheer coincidence my high school guidance counselor turned out to be a pedophile, and was arrested and convicted when I was a sophomore. When I was sixteen I was under five feet tall, and weighed in at a hefty seventy-eight pounds. My tits were tardy, and tiny. I welcomed my first pubic hair in my very late teens. Here I was, a twelve-year-old in the physical sense, and Mr. Owl never made a move. I mean, it begs the question. I've always told myself no one ever wanted me in high school because I was prepubescent for so long, but the fact that Mr. Owl never even copped an "accidental" feel makes that a little harder to fall back on. I mean, what am I supposed to tell myself?

When I got to college I did what any inexperienced, nubile virgin would do: I overcompensated. I made a habit of sneaking up on my roommate buck naked and jumping on her lap, preferably while she was wearing shorts. I gave ball gags and nipple clips as birthday gifts. I even had a squirt gun with a rubber penis-shaped barrel with which I would accost my neighbors in the elevator. Basically, I was a low-level sex offender.

I guess Mr. Owl did rub off on me a little, even if he never rubbed up against me.

By this point I had some suitors, but none that suited me. It was the new millenium, and I was twenty. I had a brand-new best pal, Tyler, out of the closet since age fifteen. He'd recently finished playing the role of Jesus in *Jesus Christ Superstar*, and we spent many afternoons contentedly watching *Ab Fab* or listening to Dar Williams, before he made his surprise move. Perhaps it was my boyish figure, or my overt penis envy—who can say? But for whatever reason, Tyler, who had never so much as glanced sidelong with lust at a lady, made an overture. I went with it.

"But he's *gay!*" you're thinking.

I ignored this fact.

"Would it be weird at school?" Tyler and I wondered.

It would. Our friends were baffled, scandalized, at times angry. Turns out, once you come out of the closet, you'd better fucking stay there. But love sees no sexual orientation, and we only had eyes for each other.

We did, however, encounter one *large* obstacle.

Tyler happened to be endowed with something that even I, with no frame of reference, understood to be a massive, mastodonic cock. A *Boogie Nights* cock. Nine and a half inches of solid, stout flesh. I can describe it as a hoagie. I can describe it as Jason Giambi's head and neck. A veiny, hulking schoolyard bully of a cock.

Here's the thing. Contrary to conventional wisdom, this is not always good news. It's especially bad news if you're a five-foot-four, ninety-five-pound virgin. How would this work? Tyler was very stressed about it. I assured him I would be fine and internalized my fears, but I knew I needed to do some stretching exercises. I needed to prep. But how? How, how, *how*?

Remember the squirt gun, guys? The one with the penis-shaped barrel?

I lost my virginity to a squirt gun.

I stuck a squirt gun up my no-no. I rolled a condom onto it and gave it my flower.

There's more.

Having left my virginity behind, I then convinced my gay boyfriend to give me *his*—five years after he came out of the closet. To set the mood, I put on the Backstreet Boys' *Millenium* album, which may be the only choice I made that night that I don't regret.

The problem was, the squirt gun I'd made love to was probably only a third the size of Tyler's dong, which just wouldn't . . . go . . . in. It just wasn't happening. I sat down on it, and it was like sitting on a bicycle seat. Uncomfortable, but exterior. It was like a barstool. So. We did what two twenty-year-old virgins—one gay, one straight—would do. We improvised.

We didn't have a lot of time; Tyler had rehearsal for *Tommy* in forty-five minutes downtown and would already need to take a cab. We didn't have any actual lube, so we threw out some ideas. Hand cream? Sunscreen? Hair gel? Hmm. Did I have any butter? Yes! Yes, I did.

So I retrieved a stick of butter from the fridge, and we copiously buttered Tyler's French roll. We buttered Tyler up and down and all around, and we gave ourselves to each other. And I will say, it was in its own way magical, on my dorm room twin bed with Nick Carter's crooning voice in the background. We laughed our way through the whole thing, and I wouldn't have it any other way, save one.

Don't use butter as lube, guys.

A couple of fun facts about butter:

1. Butter is corrosive. The butter ate right through the condom, which was then shredded around the base of Tyler's biggie-size, battered penis.

2. Butter contains bacteria. I stopped dry-heaving from the morning-after pill just in time to notice an uncomfortable sensation downtown. A vaginal infection of epic proportions.

And that's how I lost my virginity to my gay, almost-baby-daddy's nine-and-a-half-inch cock to the song stylings of the Backstreet Boys and ended up with a monster crotch infection. Except that I had already given it up to a squirt gun.

PUFF THE UN-MAGIC DRAGON

by Nick Garfinkle

I lost my virginity at sixteen, I think. The thing is, my first time happened before puberty happened.

It's August 1992. Bill Clinton isn't quite president yet, but a new day is dawning—for I'm about to have sex. She's eighteen. I'm sixteen. The state of New York calls it statutory rape. I call it "The Summer of Love." You see, I understand what the legislators of the Empire State don't—that it's theoretically impossible to take advantage of a sixteen-year-old male. (Now if the genders were reversed . . . but there's no double standard in New York.)

It's the last night of Camp Whippoorwill, and Bear Cabin is empty—probably because the director, Chip, has been too busy stealing money from the owners to do much recruiting. I bring a blanket. She brings experience. The hardwood floor is unforgiving—but I'm about to have sex! So it feels like a velvet cloud. Actually it still feels like a hardwood floor, but I'm about to have sex!

It all started one night during Awiskini, our weekly addition of insult to genocide, our "Sorry-for-the-landgrab, Native Americans, can-we-make-it-up-to-you-by-dressing-in-calfskin-ponchos-and-cribbing-your-sacred-rituals?" Or as we called it, "Friday night activity." As our council fire grew low, "Nomke the Wise" told us a story. We also painted our faces red, but the less said about that the better. She found a private moment between Circle of Truth and Indian (like we would really call it Native American) Leg Wrestling to confess, breathily, "I've been waiting two years for you to become a counselor." The laws of New York may be meaningless, but the code of Camp Whippoorwill is sacred.

And now it's time. The whole summer, our entire torrid heavy-make-out-with-a-chance-of-fondle relationship—my whole prepubescent life—has been building to this moment. She turns on her flashlight. "No, I want to do it by starlight," I say, so she won't see my worm without a hair, my snake without a lair. "But let me see your boobs first," I say, because I'm sixteen. I see them, and they are glorious, completely out of proportion with her tiny frame. Does it have something to do with her being from Wisconsin? The dairy state?

I fall on top of her, then roll us over, like I've seen that guy on the beach do in that black-and-white movie, right before they do it. I haven't seen the whole movie, but they play the roll-her-over clip at the start of coming attractions, and I assume they do it. (Note: the author has since learned that the movie is *From Here to Eternity* and that they don't actually do it, at least not on-screen.) Except I forget the guy is supposed to end up on top. But it's okay because I am a staunch supporter of women's rights! I've marched on Washington with five hundred thousand Women for Choice, my buddy Dave Panero and my mom, chanting "George Bush, stay out of my bush!" But it's no time to think about my mom's bush. She reaches into my shorts: camp-issued, elastic waistband, no resistance. And then she touches it. *No one ever touches it!* Except for me, of course, pretty much all the time, and my pediatrician, Dr. Lazarus, once a year. (He keeps promising me I'll grow hair down there. Liar.)

"It's okay," she says, "I'm on the pill." It's okay, I think, I'm incapable of producing sperm!

And then it's happening, I think. I'm not sure where exactly my bald eagle is, but it's definitely *some*where. And she's smiling, and her eyes are half-closed, so I figure it's likely. I churn my hips wildly, like that guy in that other movie, the one Dave Panero keeps hidden in his closet. I think it's happening. No, now I'm sure. I flail a rhythmless samba. She grooves an adult contemporary beat. Then she puts her lips next to my ear and whispers, "You don't have to worry about AIDS." And then I come. Air. I come air—little puffs of air from my very un-magical dragon.

I'm sixteen, and I've just lost my virginity. I think.

YOU BET YOUR ASS

by "The Flying Buttress"

This is a story about a guy named Rick. Rick and I were boyfriend and girlfriend. We made sense together in a really cool way. We were a power couple of New York's Lower East Side—dirty and shaggy, poor and rude. But we were all of those things on purpose, so we were cool.

I mean, sure, his pet name for me was "Slut," and yeah, he had a habit of sending me text messages from the toilet to tell me he was pooping, but he was really sweet and funny and would say things like, "If you ever let anyone else touch you, I'll fucking kill you." And I would think, Wow. He really loves me. Then I'd giggle and say, "Rick! You're funny!"

We had a good thing going. I introduced cool Rick to a lot of cool shit that a cool chick like me does. We did a little light B&D, we engaged in role play—I'd do a dirty nurse named Gina and sit on his face while giving him a sponge bath—and I paid plenty of attention to his balls. But Rick . . . Rick wanted more.

There's one thing I don't do. I don't give the back-lot tour. I can barely get anything to come out of there, let alone jam anything in. It's just my policy. I don't have a prostate; there's nothing in it for me. The back door's closed, boys. The back door's closed.

Rick calls it "Tiny Town."* Rick wants to go to Tiny Town. And he's relentless. He courts me with such stirring overtures as, "Just the tip, baby, just the tip." Just the tip? And *then* what? Hmm? Because I'm not letting you stick your feces-glazed "tip" in my nano.* And I'm certainly not letting you put it in my mouth. So how does this novel *end*?

I manage to hold Rick at bay until a fateful evening I convince him to come play pool with me on Bleecker Street. And we're having a blast, because billiards is *sexy*. Think about it: You're running your hands up and down a long, hard shaft of wood; you're trying to guide things into holes; there are balls bouncing around everywhere; and not least, there's a lot of bending over and presenting of the posterior. Which is almost certainly what gave Rick the idea in the first place.

Now we all know where this is headed. I *bet* my *ass*. But please be fair. It was a very safe bet. Rick was horrible at pool; I was awesome at it. He had never defeated me. And the bet proper was this: "Sure, *Rick*. If you can beat me in three consecutive games, I'll take you to Tiny Town." It was lottery odds that he'd win, and we both knew it.

And Rick didn't win. He didn't win a single game. No, Rick played predictably poorly in all three rounds. But here's where it gets fascinating. I *lost*. Three games in a row I sank every one of my balls, cleared the table, until only the eight ball remained. And I kid you not, three games in a row I scratched on the eight-ball shot. Which, to the uninitiated, is an automatic loss. Rick didn't have to beat me; I beat myself.

Three strikes. Three overconfident whiffs. Much like that poem "Casey at the Bat."

More like Casey at the butt.

I know what you may be thinking: I threw the match. Don't doubt I haven't lain awake many a night pondering,

pondering, pondering. Did I? Did I want to lose? Had I flown a kamikaze mission? Was I subconsciously a hungry bottom? Of course I wasn't. I'm no puritan, but the bottom has always been top on my "To Don't" list.

In light of that, the best hypothesis I can come up with is this: I think my asshole was jealous of my vagina. Hear me out. Here's Lisa up front—very popular, getting all the attention, all the phone calls—while all poor Alice out back gets to do is vomit shit two or three times a week. So yeah, I think, in the crucial moment, my asshole called in a favor to my brain, who in turn gave my motor skills the night off, and the more I think about it the more I believe it and think, Fuck you, asshole!

Poor choice of words.

Back to Bleecker Street. I find myself doing a dead man walking out to a cab with Rick, who's wearing a look of thrilled disbelief. He looks like a guy who's just won the teddy bear from the metal claw arcade machine—he's beaten the odds and defied physics. He's not entirely cruel—he buys me two shots of whisky (that I hope will have a numbing effect). He even offers me an out, but not because of magnanimity. It was a win-win for him. He got to be the good guy, knowing full well that I had too much pride to renege on a bet; that I would forever compromise my credibility in doing so, a credibility I prized, apparently, more highly than my virgin ass.

I don't know how many of you out there have been to Tiny Town. Market research would suggest quite a few. Anal is a mainstay of gay men, adventurous straights, and abstinence-committed teens everywhere. But, if you're an ignoranus,* like I was, be warned: It's not something to be entered into lightly, or after too large a meal. I know all you bottoms out there feel me when I say the first time you head to Tiny Town, one question predominates: When I get there, is there gonna be a mudslide?

Here's a little taste of what went on between the cheeks. My butt clenched up like a baby who won't eat his beets, but Rick gave me a good open-palm lube job and I took it—not just the tip, baby—I *took* it. How did it feel? Not good. Even with the lube it felt . . . gritty. Grainy? Kind of sandy. What was I thinking? When you're getting it in The Brown* there's no way to see if anything foul is happening . . . if anything's been loosed or jostled free. If the "locals" will be friendly to this . . . visitor. More seasoned catchers know to spring-train with an enema or at the very least a rigorous shower. I just prayed for luck. I tried to make a few sexy noises, not to be generous—just to try to move things along. Welcome to Tiny Town. Population one too many. It wasn't cool.

But I didn't shit everywhere! I didn't shit for six days.

CHAPTER 2

SELF-HELP

love thyself . . . but do it carefully.

As any book in the personal growth section will tell you, you cannot truly begin to love another until you learn how to love yourself. You would think this would be difficult to screw up. It can prove challenging, however, especially when you realize the biggest demons of all . . . may live inside. The first step in healing a dysfunctional relationship with yourself is to admit you have a problem. The second is to realize you're not alone. The stories in this chapter touch upon the self-destructive side of self-pleasure. . . .

CAUGHT DICK-HANDED

by Zach Steel

I grew up surrounded by vaginas. The only penis I ever knew was my own. I remember one day in my early childhood, years before my parents' divorce, sharing a pee with my father. I remember his huge penis, lying in the palm of his hand, emitting a thick, steady rainbow of urine next to my small penis, held between my thumb and pointer finger, casting a much thinner, very erratic stream, similar to what happens when you put your thumb over the opening of a hose. I was all over the place, hitting the front of the bowl so it would spray back a bit on our legs, then into the bowl, crossing through his stream, and up the far side of the bowl and out again, making more of a mess behind the toilet. No one was laughing. I obviously had a problem. The hole at the end of my penis is shaped like a peanut, making it very hard to control what happens with my stream. I was dancing all over the place, trying to anticipate where my pee would land by moving my feet around while angling my penis in all directions to see which combinations worked best. My father just stood there, his piss the mighty and constant baritone below my strange and arrhythmic soprano. That was it. From there on out, all vaginas.

A few years later, six vaginas and I—my mother's vagina, my three sisters' vaginas, a nanny's vagina, and a dog's vagina—all crammed into the Volvo and headed to California, leaving my father and his penis behind. The front seat looked like this: vagina vagina vagina. The backseat was like this: vagina penis vagina. That was my childhood in a Volvo, only slightly more intimate. They might not have always been sitting next to me, but they were always lurking.

Needless to say, it took me a while to figure out how to jerk off. Years and years of boners were left to their own devices to find their way back to a state of calm. To this day, I still don't know how most boys figured it out. For me, it was a matter of simulating what I thought a vagina looked like with my two hands. I put the palms of my hands together in a clap position, opened them ever so slightly, rotated the shape so my fingers pointed at the ground, and held it at crotch level. I then proceeded to hump that shape, not realizing that it would have been much easier to have moved the shape back and forth as opposed to my entire body. It wasn't long before I threw realism out the door and just went with the traditional finger donut, still humping the fixed shape. It was this technique that resulted in my first orgasm. Two soaring pearls shot out, one and then the next, and landed on the tiled wall in front of me. I stared at them, red-faced, gasping for air as they slowly worked their way down the bathroom wall, preferring the grouted lanes to the wily and slick tile surface. It was time for a shower.

I stood under the hot water, in shock, on the verge of tears over the pleasure that I had just discovered. Seconds later, I found myself at it again, only this time, slightly bored and confused. Was that it? Did I break it? Why is it so red and tingly? Do I have to wait? How long? I had to find out. During this shower—a shower of fury and bewilderment—I discovered the incredible ecstasy my swift and dexterous arm muscles could produce. While maintaining stillness in the rest of my body, my pelvis severely tucked under and my toes spread wide and tensed upward, I attacked myself, ferociously jutting my finger donut back and forth and back and forth around me. Imagine this in slow motion, because otherwise you won't be able to see it. Within the hour, I had revived that tired snake and produced another one and a half not-so-heaven-bound pearls of joy. As I watched those cream worms slither down the drain, maintaining their constitution even after a gentle toeing, I decided it was time for a break. I had made my case. I began my regimen of two-a-days.

I kept this pace for the next few years, one session in my morning shower, one before I went to sleep, and a midday workout thrown in every so often. Rarely did I let the gift of a boner go without a proper how-do-you-do. It was never easy, though. Women and girls abounded in my home, and I had to work for my successes, waking up a half hour earlier, staying up later, covering my tracks like a criminal. I *was* a criminal.

The bathroom was my main location. I shared a room with my younger sister, so that was rarely available, and every other room in the house had street-level windows, so to be safe I just stayed in the bathroom. Even so, I had to remain quiet. The bathroom was attached to my other two sisters' rooms, and they were light sleepers. I took precautions. I always released into the sink—easy cleanup and no *plop* when my ejaculate hit the surface. I always faced a wall so that my body would deflect the sound waves from going under the door and into the bedrooms. This positioning was also a safeguard against anyone walking in, so they would only see my butt, and I could start crying or something so they would think I was just going through some shit, not necessarily masturbating. After all, how would they know what boys did when they masturbated, and if it differed from what they did when they were just going through some shit?

Then one day, something amazing happened. I was doing my thing in the corner of the bathroom when I heard something coming from the house next door—a rhythmic springboard jostling coupled with earthy moaning. I covered myself up and walked out into the kitchen. The sound was overwhelming. A couple living directly on the other side of the kitchen wall were fucking like grizzly bears. I could hear everything: the bed hitting the wall, the passionate moaning, crotches slamming together. I was consumed. Blood was rushing everywhere. They were getting louder and louder. I whipped it out and went to work right there in the kitchen. I came wherever. I took a moment, cleaned up my work, and then scurried off to bed, never hearing the climax from next door, although I'm sure it happened. I didn't know who these people were. I didn't know what they looked like. Maybe a whore lived there, and it was a different guy every night. Maybe they were two four-hundred-pounders with moles and wounds all over their junk. I didn't care. All I knew was that beautiful things were happening next door, and I owed my life to these animals.

I officially changed my main location. Yes, it was riskier because there was no door to protect me on one side, but if I ever heard anyone coming, I could just pretend I was looking for a late-night snack and hide my erection in the refrigerator while acting absolutely appalled by anything happening next door. That never happened. Sometimes I would spend hours in the kitchen waiting for the next-door neighbors to start me up, and no one ever walked in on me. I guess I was the only member of the household with a late-night agenda.

I was gaining confidence. The house was mine. I was like a werewolf, but instead of turning into a wolf at night, I jerked off a lot. I was like a night watchman, but instead of sitting at a hotel desk all night, I jerked off in my kitchen. One of my sisters had gone off to college, uncluttering the house by a small percentage. My mother started working more, which meant she slept harder, which meant the nights were longer, which meant more time for me and the neighbors.

Tragically the next-door sex slowed down and then eventually came to a complete stop. My muses had departed; I needed something to fill the void, and soon. I couldn't go back to staring at the bathroom wall. That would be too painful. I needed to move forward, conquer new rooms, new inspiration. I tried jerking off in other rooms, in other chairs, lying down on the floor. It all felt empty. It was fine, but that's it. I needed something else.

Porn. Porn was what I needed. For some reason, I had always thought of porn as something you watch with a group of friends in awkward silence while trying to push your boner down. It never crossed my mind how enjoyable it would be to watch by yourself. Maybe it was because the only TV in the house was in the living room, which had a floor-to-ceiling bay window that looked directly out onto the street. It was risky, but I had to try it. Something had to change.

So I stole a video from one of my friends and made plans to watch it that night. I got intermittent boners the entire day thinking about what I was going to do to myself. I carried the video around all day in school, and every so often would sneak a peak at the cover and get a quick boner. The image was of a massive orgy with middle-aged men and women splayed about various bearskin rugs, scratching each other and showing their teeth. It was called *Wet Fur* or something. This was going to be extra special.

Night fell and I waited silently in bed for my sisters to go to sleep, then crept to my location. The moon shone through the bay window and cast a cold light upon the room, so I didn't need to turn on any lights. Perfect. Yes, I was exposed to the street, but who walked down our street at this hour anyway? I turned on the television and quickly turned the volume down. No volume. No, sir. I popped the video in and quickly fast-forwarded through the dialogue. There it was. Bonertime. I decided to take off all my clothes to really get down with myself. I sat on the floor, Indian-style, next to the couch to partially shield myself from the street. The TV, though, was completely visible. I was beginning to enjoy the danger. Like people who have sex after car crashes, the danger was turning me on. And so what if someone walked by? It's not like they would tap on the glass and tell me to stop. If I didn't turn around to see them, then they didn't exist.

On the TV, everyone was fucking everything. There were blowjobs, hand jobs, fingerings, licking, slamming, jamming, people putting it in the back door, keys jingling in the front door, door opening, my sister staring at me, me picking up the remote and taking way too long to find the pause button, and then whoosh. Silence. My sister and I staring at each other, bathed in the blue light that poured from the TV. I stood up for some reason.

"Zach," she said, disappointed.

"Sorry?" I said.

It was the older one from college. I had forgotten she was coming home for spring break. She was unaccounted for, and I was too obsessed with the bay window to even consider the front door. There were too many vaginas to keep track of. I couldn't avoid them forever. They would always be sitting right next to me even as I jerked off. It made me wonder if there had been other times that I had been caught and not even known about it. Maybe when I was in the kitchen listening to the neighbors, one of them might have walked in and I was too focused on my work to notice. This was the end of a glorious time in my life. A carefree, anything-goes-on-whatever-surface-in-any-room-in-the-house time of my life. Good-bye.

Epilogue:

Yeah, I still jerk off. But it's not the same. I got caught a couple more times in college by various roommates because I was just being stupid. The game is no longer fun. I live with my fiancée, who has caught me a few times but doesn't even care. She just continues doing whatever she was doing. Am I invisible, for God's sake?

A CUSHION FOR THE PUSHIN'

by Michael J. Nice

Like all good stories about teenage masturbation, my story begins with my grandmother. My grandmother lived with us in a separate in-law apartment attached to our house. Mo-Mo, as we called her, was slightly crippled from a pommel horse accident back when she was in high school. It was the 1940s, and they didn't have the proper hip realignment technology to fix the problem, so from that day forward, my grandmother walked with a limp. She would correct the limp by wearing one normal shoe, and one giant Super-Freak Pimp Shoe.

Because of her handicap, Mo-Mo always had to be propped up wherever she sat. On the sofa, a cushion would be placed under the existing cushion to give Mo some additional lift. Getting her into a comfortable seated position was like molding a horse out of Play-Doh; it's going to stand effectively for a minute, but as time goes by, it will eventually droop and become unrecognizable.

Mo-Mo's daybed was no exception. While watching *The People's Court*, Mo would adjust and prop herself up using what we referred to in my house as "bolsters." They weren't sofa cushions as much as they were elongated foam tube cushions. They were roughly three feet long, a foot and a half high, and maybe ten inches deep.

Meanwhile, I was a weird kid. I was a sexually confused fourteen-year-old with what I would call a slightly above-average libido. I would masturbate between two and thirty-seven times a day. One day, while Mo and my mom were out shopping, I was relaxing between my 2:15 jerk-off and my 2:23 jerk-off by watching some TV. I got to snuggling with one of those bolsters. I had never held another human in a sexual manner, so the experience of embracing something roughly as large as myself and getting an erection was new to me. This was a new frontier. I held the cushion tight and thrust my groin into it. I began to dry hump my grandmother's back-support bed cushion.

I stopped myself to assess the situation. Could this cushion be smuggled to my bedroom so further experimentation could occur? I immediately concluded that yes, it could; yes, it should; and yes, it would. I smuggled the cushion off to my bedroom. I was ferocious with my newfound love doll. It wasn't long after that I figured out that unzipping the fabric coverlet and dry humping the foam cushion inside was the way to go. And then the ultimate filthy, adolescent, sexual revelation: I realized that I could, quite realistically (or so I thought), simulate sex with an actual human being by slicing a slit, if you will, into the foam. This slit was then filled with Lubriderm skin care lotion; I mean, it had the word "lube" right in it. I was good to go. Sexual intercourse with an inanimate object was now within my horny grasp. Genius! I thought. I had become a perverted little Dr. Frankenstein, and the cushion was my sex monster.

My affair with the cushion lasted several months. I would sneak the cushion into my room, have my way with it, and return it, cleaned (for the most part), and no one was the wiser.

But as the weeks dragged on, my relationship with the cushion became strained. I couldn't put forth the effort to drag that thing up to my bedroom, fuck it, clean it, and then return it to my grandmother's bed. And I was mortified by the thought of ever being caught. Worse yet, what if, while cleaning the coverlet, my filthy fuck hole was discovered in the cushion? There was only one course of action. The cushion had to be eliminated.

And so, exhibiting the characteristics of a budding serial killer, I kidnapped my fuck-doll-cushion-thing after sunset one night and dragged it to a wooded area not far from my house. It saddened me that it had to end this way, but I knew this was the only way it could end. I took one last look at my first regular sex partner, threw it down, and covered it with sticks and leaves. I nodded a satisfied nod as I took my final glance, before turning and running off, knowing it was for the best.

No one ever questioned the whereabouts of that sofa cushion, and for a time I thought I'd gotten away with the perfect crime. Until the day came when my mom arrived home with a new set of cushions for Mo, and her first words to me were, "And Michael, you keep your grubby hands off these ones." I'm still not clear exactly what she meant by that.

CHAPTER 3

RELATIONSHIT*

why the committed sometimes
ought to be committed

Ah, l'amour. *You meet that special someone and breathe
a huge sigh of relief—the hard part's over! Think again.
The ins and outs of a relationship can lay bare monogamy's
monsters: expectations, jealousy, dependency, insanity.
The pressures of love can test even the strongest of unions:
Adam and Eve, Catherine and Heathcliff, Pepé Le Pew and
the cat . . . sometimes it just stinks. Whether it's the type of bond
that even death cannot destroy, or one you were not even
aware you were in to begin with (poor cat), sexual missteps
often take on greater significance with a significant other.*

HOW HE BECAME MY NUMBER ONE BY TAKING CARE OF MY NUMBER TWO

by Erin Pineda

I'm a very lucky girl. I have fallen madly in love. His name is Steven, and he is the kindest man I have ever met. He is my better half, he is my soul mate, and all that crap. Which brings me to my story. We were blissfully happy up until a few weeks ago, when we moved in together.

You see, during the entire course of our relationship I have never pooed in front of, in back of, or anywhere near Steven. I have refrained from all things scatological. So much so that this conversation actually occurred:

Steven: "You don't poop."

Me: "No. I don't poop."

Steven: "Where does it go?"

Me: "Um . . . it evaporates."

Steven: "What?"

Me: "You know, kind of like photosynthesis."

I don't remember what photosynthesis is exactly, but it sounded plausible. More importantly, I got Steven to stop talking about "number two."

Now, you're probably wondering why I put so much effort into hiding my deuces. Many people would argue that it's human, and therefore beautiful. It's what connects us all. *Everybody Poops*, right? But not so much when it comes to love, especially romantic love. Poop and all its cousins—diarrhea, farts, and sharts—don't really fan the flames of passion or ignite the fires of desire, no matter how many matches you light.

In college my boyfriend decided it would be cute if I started tooting in front of him. I obliged and let 'em rip. He labeled them "low rumblers" and broke up with me less than a month later.

My relationship directly before Steven was based largely on a student/teacher dynamic; he was a much older man who was accomplished and distinguished, and I was really horny and easy. In essence he turned me out and not too much later turned me off. It happened one day in a phone conversation when he informed me in great detail about an epic bout of diarrhea he caught while traveling to Greece.

"I'm peeing water!" he exclaimed. Which I thought was a good thing, until he said it was coming out of his ass. Sex was never the same.

Which brings us up to date. I had succeeded in maintaining sexual desirability with Steven by a complete absence of doody. According to him I was clean and pure, like a lily. And then came moving day, and a whole bunch of grapes. And granola. And then coffee. I just *had* to poo! I thought to myself, I can't hide this forever; we live together! This is my place too! I should, I would, and, heaven almighty, I could!

And I did. Oh my God I did. It was like the dam had broken, and a year's worth of self-repression burst through, and I felt good; I felt light and I felt free and then I flushed. . . .

The poo would not go down.

I fought with the poo for half an hour, pleading with it, imploring it, trying desperately to rid myself, the apartment, and Steven of my shameful baggage. I even recited three Hail Marys, to which I knew only the first line, and flushed again. But the waters began to rise. Would the levees hold? There was only one person I could turn to.

So a few moments later I faced what I had worked for years to avoid. Down the hall and a little to the right, my boyfriend was plunging my poo. I hid under the blankets, leaving him alone to wrestle with the monster. I couldn't watch. He was face-to-face with my inner demons, a part of me only my mother had seen. Laid out before him was evidence of the mess I could make. I heard him holler from the bathroom, "A log is resurfacing!" Is that a good thing, I wondered?

I started planning for what would of course be the end of our relationship. He would break up with me in the next few days. I'd probably move in with my friend Ross; he has two bathrooms, and one even has a fan. Losing Steven would be painful, but I would survive. I'd be a shell of a person, but . . .

No. No, I can't think like that. I will not accept defeat so easily. He is the love of my life, and I will fight for him.

So after I heard a flush and Steven's voice proclaim, "Hooray! Bye, poo!" I called him into the bedroom and did what any desperate, humiliated girl would do. I started touching myself and talking dirty.

"My pussy is wet," I told him.

"So is the bathroom floor," he replied.

I ignored this and writhed around on the bed, grabbing my bathing suit parts. He stood nearby, looking at me like I was a three-legged dog, a pitiful creature. He suggested I take a shower. A long one.

I wondered if he was inferring that I had crapped all over myself, which I found a bit patronizing. But I let it go, figuring he had been through enough. When I got out of the shower, I found him passed out on the bed; like kryptonite, my excrement had weakened him. But I was not about to let this go, so I turned on my "sexy times" playlist and saddled up.

But everything was different. His hands were tentative, careful, especially around my derriere. I sensed avoidance. I made a move to flip over, but he delicately held me in place, resisting doggy styling. My mind was spinning; was he looking at me through poo-colored glasses?

The sex was boring. It was the kind old married people have, or Republicans. And because I was having that with *him*, it was the worst sex I'd ever experienced. So I decided to step it up and really go for the gold. I started humping him desperately. After the third or fourth time he said "ouch," I eased up.

His penis looked like Sylvester Stallone at the end of *Rocky*—his one good eye swollen shut. Finally, in a soft, polite voice he asked, "Erin, could we please stop?"

I felt like sobbing. "Of course we can, sweetheart," I said, and he conked out. I lay there next to him and wept into my pillow.

The next morning I woke up early to try to catch him, but he had already headed to work. I was miserable and angry. I even refused to drink my morning coffee, believing it was the evil catalyst that had doomed my relationship. I swore to myself to always take anti-diarrheal medicine and maintain constipation for eternity. Never again would anyone see the monsters inside of me, and never again would I go to the bathroom in anyone's presence; from now on I would keep my shit to myself.

But right now I was alone, so . . .

I walked into the bathroom and went to sit on the toilet, but something caught my eye. There in the bowl, like a pot of gold at the end of a rainbow, was the kindest, most loving gift anyone could have ever offered. There was Steven's poo. He had left his shit out for me to see, unguarded, uncovered, vulnerable. So that morning, happily, fearlessly, I plunged his poo.

To this day he claims it was left there because he was in a rush and forgot to flush. But I know the real reason. He was making a point: When you truly love someone, you have to deal with each other's shit.

And now I can again happily envision our future: waking up on a Sunday morning, enjoying breakfast in bed, loading up the minivan, and dropping our kids off at the pool . . . together.

MY FAST BOYFRIEND

by Mary Lynn Rajskub

I was wearing extra-large green army shorts, a large white T-shirt, black suspenders, very short hair, red lipstick, and, of course, combat boots. Sex was not really something I was advertising; nevertheless, this was the look that drew Todd to me like a foxy magnet. I was treading water sexually and personally. I had no confidence and only a very limited sense of street style. He said he thought I was a very cute lesbian—a lipstick lesbian! Todd had longish hair, a southern California accent, and a chunk of wood in his ear, stretching it out like an aboriginal citizen of the world. He's a free thinker, I thought, and super unique. Todd also mentioned that he wrote poetry. We were perfect for each other. This was very exciting indeed.

It turned out we were meant to be together even more than I thought. I worked at Double Rainbow ice cream, and he worked four doors down at the Good Earth grocery store. He cares about the environment and works at an organic health food store to prove it. I have got to get to know this guy, I said to myself. So I immediately invited him over to the apartment I shared with my roommate, Sharon. Sharon agreed to cook her now-famous eggplant Parmesan, which she had never cooked before, but I'll tell you it was delicious—very thin, baked cheese browned on the top, and perfectly cooked to the bottom of the pan. I should've known something was wrong when he didn't eat it. How could someone not like Sharon's eggplant? It was so delicious. I guess I forgot, because twenty minutes after dinner, I was showing him the rooftop of our apartment, and we began to furiously make out. Todd fell on top of me, pushing me down in an incredibly passionate way. I know it was passionate because my back was being ground into the gravel and I still continued to make out. This was very exciting to me. This was what I wanted in life: romance, excitement, vibrancy.

Soon after, Todd was pushing me around and making out forcefully with me every chance he got. One particular afternoon, while I was the only salesperson working at Double Rainbow, he pushed me into the back office, pressing his tongue into my mouth. Yes, I thought, this is how it's supposed to be. Except—wait a minute—I wasn't enjoying this at all. In fact, the real me was floating up near the ceiling trying to get the attention of my body. What are you doing? the bodiless me tried to yell. Stop! This isn't fun!

You're right, it's not, I thought back. But, hold on, shut up. This is my fast-track romance; I've got to get into this quickly or else I'm going to miss the boat. This guy digs me, and he cares about the environment. I need this. He supports Food Not Bombs, and that says it all right there. I think they feed the homeless. He has stretched out his ear by wearing a wood chip in it—that shows commitment. This guy knows what passion is. I have got to get with the program or else San Francisco will chew me up and spit me out.

I got it together and pretended to be super into the make-out, although all I was thinking was, This is gross, and what if a customer comes in?

The next time we had sex, Todd informed me that he was going to get his penis pierced, but not to worry because it was for my sexual enhancement, as well as his own. He didn't even ask; he just told me. I guessed this was what a progressive relationship was all about. It seemed like an asshole move, but I thought maybe he knew something I didn't. It would take eight weeks to heal. We'd just started dating, and now we couldn't have sex for eight weeks. And then I'd get to have some weird shit stuck in my body.

During the waiting period, Todd called me late at night and asked me if I wanted to go on a walk. Oh, he wants to see me! I thought. He still wants to see me, and he's had to consider the fact that his penis won't be going in me. He must really like me. Well, we went on a walk starting at midnight; Todd rode his skateboard and I walked behind. Then he would stop and wait for me to catch up, and then I'd end up walking behind him again. We continued like this for three or four hours. I just wanted to see what was going to happen and how long it would go on. I had become quite used to walking in the city, even at night, but I had never done anything like this before. When we finally headed back, I asked him how he could walk this far, and he said, "Oh, I'm on speed."

"Really? Oh."

That was pretty much the end of the discussion. I wondered if this could explain some of the stuff that seemed strange to me. The hyperactive making out and the fact that sometimes Todd seemed to be crawling out of his skin, or not wanting to be touched at all. Knowing this about him made me want to break up, but he didn't seem to think it was a big deal, so I didn't make a big deal of it.

When his penis finally healed, Todd invited me over to unveil his proud possession.

"Look! Isn't it fantastic?"

"It really is something! Wow!"

This is when things started to get really weird. He started hanging objects from his penis and wanted me to start hanging more and more things from it. I frantically looked through his room. A pair of scissors? Sure! Paper clips? Okay! A pen? Go ahead and try. When we ran out of things to hang from his penis, Todd removed the belt from his pants.

"Hit me with the belt," he told me.

"Really?"

"Yes."

So I did. Again and again I hit him with the belt. I have to admit, it was pretty fun, and it made him very excited. It wasn't what I would call intimate, and I wondered if it would be like this every time from now on. Maybe if I was open to his sexual needs, I thought, we would become close.

After sex, Todd proceeded to the kitchen and started to make a healthy vegetarian stew. It was my job to cut up the celery. Suddenly he became angry.

"You're wasting the vegetable," he said, commenting on the fact that I didn't use the entire stalk. Wow, he really doesn't want to waste a scrap of food, I thought. Maybe he's doing speed for the environment, so he can consume less. What a guy!

The next time I saw Todd, which was about a week later, I expected that we would get the band back together for some penis decorating. Then I noticed that he had hickeys all over his neck. And so I asked, "Are those hickeys?" He looked at me like I was the most intrusive person on the planet. He waited about thirty seconds, staring at me in disgust, then finally answered, "My ex-girlfriend and I got back together."

A BEDTIME STORY

by Laraine Newman

It was the early 1970s. I was in the improv group The Groundlings, but we hadn't named ourselves yet. That's where I met Greg. He was gorgeous, funny, and sweet. For our first date, I invited him over to my apartment for dinner. I was going to make beef Stroganoff. I thought myself to be an intuitive cook, so I didn't really follow any kind of recipe. I just used a lot of butter, and if I do say so myself, it tasted delicious.

The dinner was going great. He liked my cooking, and we were making each other laugh. But that went from being a good thing, to being a very, very bad thing. Because at one point, I was laughing so hard that I peed in my pants. Now, I was sitting in one of those wooden chairs that are hollowed out to fit the contours of your ass and legs. Once that had filled up with pee, the urine was then flowing over the sides of the chair and pounding onto the floor like Niagara Falls. I'm telling you it was loud. I was certain he could hear it, but he didn't. As the laughter died down I was like a deer in the headlights trying to figure out what to say. I was paralyzed. There was no way I could hide this. I had to come clean, so to speak. I selected the least indelicate word to describe my condition, and with all the courage I could muster I said, "Greg, I have voided." Greg just laughed and said "It's hard to keep up, isn't it?" He took this to mean that I had no rejoinder for the last funny thing he said. That I couldn't top it.

I was fucked. Confessing the truth felt like that moment
of regret right before you plummet to the ground on Freefall
at Six Flags Magic Mountain. It had taken every ounce of
my resolve to jump off that cliff and tell him the *first* time. I
wasn't going to do it again. I was in some kind of existential
Lucy Ricardo nightmare.

Finessing a cursory mop-up while backing out of the room
like a geisha and then making a dash for the bathroom to
change seemed about as daunting a task as trying to get from
one place to another in one of those *Resident Evil* movies. The
thought of being discovered at any point during that maneu-
ver felt like death. But that's exactly what I did.

Without a word, and in a matter of twenty seconds, I
bolted upright, grabbed a dishcloth, soaked up what I could,
threw the limp and dripping thing in the sink, and ran *backward* down the hall into the bathroom, all the while engag-
ing in a banter I only prayed would misdirect his attention.
Having made it to the bathroom, the only article of clothing I could change into was my nightgown, which was hanging on the door. I had to be fast. I didn't want there to be
enough time for him to discover the remaining pool of piss on
the kitchen floor. I frantically dried myself with a towel, then
dusted myself with scented talc to try and camouflage the
unmistakable tang I was certain was wafting off me. I pulled
the nightgown on, and the fact that it was made out of a jer-
sey material combined with the fact that I was still damp
made a once pretty but by no means sexy nightie turn into a
wet T-shirt version of Elvira's floor-length gown.

I wasn't aware of that until I emerged from the bathroom

like I was shot out of a cannon. It didn't occur to me how peculiar it might look that halfway through the meal, I was suddenly dressed for bed. Greg looked at me standing there. No words passed between us, but the expression on his face said, "Okay, I don't know you that well, but I like you and the beef Stroganoff was great, even though I'm not finished eating and I'm still awful hungry. But I really like the way that . . . uh . . . floor-length T-shirt gown is clinging to you. Doesn't leave much to the imagination."

He thought I was seducing him! To my horror, at that moment, it dawned on me that if he laid a hand on my naked flesh, I'd still be moist, with tinkle!

Instead of walking toward Greg into the kitchen, I did a sharp, Snagglepuss "exit stage left" detour into the living room. I dropped to the floor and started rolling back and forth, trying to wick the wee-wee from the back of my legs. Greg was right behind me.

So, not only did he see me drop suddenly to the floor, he saw me inexplicably tossing myself from side to side. Now, let's review. The dinner is going fine, and then suddenly I have backed out of the kitchen while mopping something off the floor. Something he's not bothered to question or investigate. I've changed clothes. Right in the middle of the meal, I've changed into a nightgown with no natural segue. Now I'm writhing on the floor. But Greg didn't question any of this.

In fact, with a wry smile on his face, he knelt down to kiss me! I tried to dodge the kiss, but we ended up head-butting as we both tried to stand up. I'm not kidding when I tell you that the sound was exactly like two coconuts. This cracked up both of us. I grabbed his hand and led him into the bathroom and turned on the shower. There was going to be a clean and soapy frolic before the big moment.

The sex was great, and minutes after I was certain he was asleep, I crept into the kitchen to make sure there was no further trace of proof at the crime scene. Conscience clear, I fell blissfully asleep, but around three in the morning I awoke to sounds coming from the bathroom: groaning, farting. "Oh, Jesus Christ, ahhh. Oh man . . . ahh, ooo. Oh awww."

After twenty minutes of this, a mortified and thoroughly ashen Greg staggered back into the bedroom.

"I think the beef Stroganoff was a little rich. Christ, did you hear any of that?"

I lay in bed with the pillow jammed against my mouth so he wouldn't hear how hard I was laughing. When I finally came up for air I said, "You know, Greg, growing up in my household, we thought farting was an art form. I'm just sorry I poisoned you."

In the landscape of bodily function humiliation, what he went through was vastly more embarrassing than pissing oneself. And the amazing thing is, my fountain of shame was a christening of sorts. For indeed, my friends, this first date was the beginning of our two-year relationship.

Soon afterward, he moved in. Within a minute he pulled out a pipe and strutted around my apartment like he owned the place. It was then that I began to consider new ways to poison him.

Decades later, when my daughters were younger, but old enough to hear an, um, sanitized version of this story, it became their favorite and one they would beg for at bedtime by chanting, "Beef Stroganoff story, Beef Stroganoff story."

"Oh . . . all right."

HONG KONG BOTTOM

by Jay Janson

My mother's chemo brought on many side effects: She wouldn't eat for anyone, her legs looked like tree trunks, and her son hooked up with a needy gaysian.* Mom got better and bounced back like a motherfucker, but me? I'm still paying for the wrath of the Hong Kong bottom.

I'm a flying solo kind of guy. Not many friends, not a social butterfly; as long as I have some time to write a few chapters of my novel, I'm kicking it easy in the NYC. But life turned ugly when my mom got sick, and for the first time ever, I felt alone.

Word to the wise, if you're a good-looking gay who needs some comfort: Hug a pillow, pat a puppy, drink detox tea, and breathe. . . . *Do not reveal your pain to a twink!*

I met Julian at my work. I was his waiter. He was a bold gay, dining alone in D&G head to toe to purse. He was a cross between Sanjaya and the middle Jonas brother, if the Jonas Brothers were Taiwanese. A fresh twenty-one, and new to the city, Julian wanted to celebrate. A mixed-green salad and two cosmos later, we planned to meet up after my shift. I'm not a mover-and-shaker, and haven't been twenty-one for, oh, about a decade. But when he said how beautiful my eyes were, I thought to myself, Think beyond "I only date bears";* why not try a soft-spoken Asian? He seemed polite and sweet; the kind of upbeat I'd been aching for.

I love me a good margarita, and after four of them, Julian

got my life story as it stood. Mom has cancer. I fly home every month to help out. I love Patron Silver. Julian was moved by my situation, as he sipped his third cosmo through a straw.

He leaned over and said, "I want to take care of you tonight," trailing his nervous fingers 'cross my thirty-something cheek.

I'm not a tender type, and a gesture like that would ordinarily have crossed my PDA boundaries. But I was vulnerable, and decided to let Julian "take care of me" the best he could. Hopeful translation: Give up that ass to some broken-hearted inches.

When we got to my apartment it was clothes off, cocks out, and a nice stick of incense. He sucked my dick so hard I tasted iron in my mouth, like blood was going to burst from my nose. I'm a bashful peaker, but something about the way Julian swirled and twirled my downtown-precious made me feel like the "Man in the Mirror." And I about *changed* all over his face.

"Oh, fuck. Sorry man."

"It's okay," Julian sighed. "I guess this means we're boyfriends, right?"

Memories of my Vietnam-vet uncle telling me Asian girls move fast so they can get that ticket to America filled my mind.

"Whoa. Take it easy, okay?"

"What does *that* mean?"

"It means we met five hours ago. Let's play it by ear . . . okay?"

"Whatever . . . jerk."

And so began the roles game. And our "relationship." I

talk honestly; I'm the *man*. He pouts openly; he's the *woman*. Psychologically, I am not equipped to deal with anything feminine in a sexual scenario; it really makes no sense to me. So, if a guy I hook up with instantly identifies himself as a blushing geisha desperate to please her man, I'm done. Call me a prick, call me a player, but I have no interest in a straight woman's mind games. Don't make me have to think about what a blowjob means if you expect to hear from me again.

But I was in a sad state; the idea of waking up next to someone made me feel like a normal person. So I said the two words I knew I'd regret.

"I'm sorry."

"I know, baby. I know." Before my eyes could roll, he tipped that ass in my direction like the green-means-go power bottom I kind of thought he was.

I pulled out my bag of free lube and condoms every gay earns when they get that AIDS test, and started checking their expiration dates. But when I finally found a Trojan with an '09 shelf life, a timid whisper came from the bed.

"You think I'm easy, don't you?"

Yes. "No." *Sigh*.

"Because I'm not. I just really, I don't know, this is a big step for me. And I don't want to get hurt. Because, well, I think I might be falling in love with you. What do you think about that?"

It was like I was trying to fuck my prom date, and her purity ring wouldn't let her go all the way. So I said what every bonehead high school kid says to get his first pair of panties.

"Me too."

Worked like a teen pregnancy charm. If I had been deaf, this would've been legendary, post-Stonewall anal, but I'm a hearing man, and when I heard "I want to take care of you, I need to take care of you" screamed over and over in a pitch as high as Mariah's early power ballads, I shriveled with every thrust. To stay hard, I thought of my holy trinity: Marc Singer in *The Beastmaster*, Harry Hamlin in *Clash of the Titans*, early *Columbo*. But then, it suddenly hit me: This Hong Kong bottom doesn't know who these people are; he wasn't even born yet. Why am I working this May/December shame spiral? There is only one Pia Zadora, and that ain't me. I have to put a stop to this! (After I come, of course. *Fair is fair.*)

The courtesy shower afterward felt like soft-core lesbian porn. He scrubbed my back lightly, dripped water from a sponge down my ass, and washed my hair with lots of suds and giggles. After we dried off and went back to the bedroom, he pulled out a DVD from his purse.

"This is my favorite movie ever. If you're going to be my boyfriend, you have to *love it! I'm totally serious!*"

Two hard cocks in a bed watching *Hairspray the Musical*. Can life get any worse?

I didn't sleep at all that night. Julian held me so tight, the morning after I had gay-hand welts all over my person. As I sat drinking my coffee, Julian put his head in my lap, and pulled my right arm away from my cup, forcing me to hold him. Nobody touches my morning Sanka; I now had grounds to break a heart.

"Yeah, you know what? This isn't going to work out. You need to go."

"Are you breaking up with me?"

"What—?" *Oh, fuck it.* "Yes. I'm breaking up with you."

And with that, he slapped me in the face and left my apartment screaming, *"Jay is gay! Jay is gay!"* as if Fred Phelps was nearby, looking to smoke out the local fag and burn him down. I live in Chelsea, NYC, not Hicktown, USA. *We all gay!*

In the weeks that followed, I heard from savvy online friends that Julian not only wrote a blog called "The Scum in New York City," but also posted my name, face, and work location as one of the most hazardous wastes out there. I didn't know he was creative.

About a year later, life was great. Mom was in total remission, I booked a commercial, and I fucked a porn star. All blessings, in their own right. One night of barhopping found me at some random gay club. In a sea of American Apparel V-neck T's and colored denim, my eyes locked onto the one and only Julian. He was dancing to Beyoncé's "Single Ladies" with a bunch of twink models, throwing hand signals like they were running a limp-wrist competition. Julian saw me, and when Beyoncé called for all the single ladies, he pointed and sang to himself, as if he were liberated from my heinous power. To the left, to the left, Beyoncé bottom—you have cock-n-balls; you ain't a single lady.

Now, look. We all have a touch o' crazy; that's what makes us special. But Julian, once again, took it one step further. As I left the club that night, I felt familiar nervous-fingers tapping on my shoulder. It was Julian, hyped up on Sasha Fierce-ness.

"I just want to let you know, I am *so* over you."

Silence.

"But we could be friends, I guess."

No response.

"And I still want to take care of you, okay? There, I said it!"

Nothing.

"Can I come over?"

Walking away.

"You bastard!"

Until we meet again.

If you have real problems in your life and you need some sort of comfort, take my advice: Jerk off.

PIE IN THE SKY

by Adria Tennor Blotta

My worst sexual experience happened when I was twenty-two . . . and lasted for four and a half years. I met Evan at a restaurant in Brooklyn where I was working as a coat check girl.

Evan was a waiter there and ten years my senior. He was quite possibly . . . no, actually, most definitely, the hottest guy who'd ever asked me out.

When he called me—well, actually he didn't call, he just walked over to the coat check—he said, "Hoh hoh hoh! When are we going to dinner?" (He talked like that, like Yogi Bear.)

After we made the date, I ran to the back of the coat closet and buried my head in a red sheared mink and screamed at the top of my lungs, *"Oh my God! I've got a date with a hot guy!"*

Evan took me out to a restaurant in Manhattan. He had three Tanqueray and tonics before dinner, and I learned that he was an ex-model turned valet driver turned waiter who was contemplating architecture school. He had two *more* Tanqueray and tonics and a glass of wine during dinner, and told me that he had ended a five-year relationship with a successful supermodel and Meatloaf video star who made six figures a year because he "just couldn't see himself with her." After dinner he took me home and walked me to my door. I thought he was being polite. He thought he was coming in.

Standing on my doorstep, I knew that if Evan came up it would be to have drunken sex, and I was just twenty-two, from the Midwest, and only wanted to have sex with someone I really loved who was also sober, at least for the first time. So Evan did not come up that night or any night during the three weeks we dated.

At the end of that three weeks, he explained to me in his white waiter jacket next to a ficus tree lit with tiny, insipid white lights that we were "not on the same sexual level." I took that to mean that my level was lower than his level, like I was the mezzanine at the MoMA or something, but isn't that where Monet's *Water Lilies* is hung?

Not to be deterred, I began wearing my cutest, sexiest outfits to check coats, and within three more weeks two things happened: Evan asked me out again and I fell madly in love with him. . . . So, we did it.

The first time was awkward. I didn't . . . you know. He did, but that's normal, right? The second time was a different story. We had a romantic dinner, then I slithered into something sexy, and . . . Evan fell asleep. The third time he fell asleep again. The fourth time, which was really the second time, was a lot like the first time: awkward, and I didn't . . . you know. He did, and actually most of the time when he didn't conk out on me, our sex was void of any effort on his part to please me.

So I moved in with him. I thought if we lived together it would get better. It didn't, and I started to grow resentful of Evan's indifference to my . . . you know. Actually, indifference isn't even the right word; he was more like completely oblivious, until finally I stopped pouting and screwed up my courage and confronted him.

"Evan, how come when we have sex . . . How come you don't, you know, make an effort to, you know . . . make me . . . you know?!"

He leaned over and adjusted the volume on the radio.

"Is this Van Halen?"

"Evan!"

"Well, I don't know. I just thought . . . I mean, it's not like you never—"

"No, it's not like never, but hardly ever, and if it was never, that might mean that there was something wrong with me, but there isn't, or that you don't know how, but you do, but you don't, which is worse."

The next night, Evan went out with his friend Charlie and came home drunk. He subtly tried to initiate sex with me by taking off his pants and waving his . . . you know, in my face. I thought maybe our conversation had gotten through to him and he wanted to redeem himself. No such luck.

"Evan, what is the problem?"

"Well, Charlie and I discussed it, and women just naturally don't have as many orgasms as men."

"What? Why would you listen to anything Charlie says? Charlie hasn't had a girlfriend or a job in over six years! Haven't you ever heard of multiple orgasms, Evan? Well, who do you think has them? Larry King?"

"It's not *my* fault if you don't . . . you know."

"Really? But if I do, you're extremely quick to take credit for it."

"Well, *yeah!*"

He fell asleep. The next morning he woke up—no, sprung

up—smiling like he'd won the lottery and took me by the shoulders in the bed and shouted.

"You're a genius! I had this dream. It was like that Tom Robbins novel, *Skinny Legs and All*, only instead of a spoon, a dirty sock, and a can o' beans, there was this big, huge, pulsing *vagina* in the sky! And oh my God! It was beautiful! Glistening! Gorgeous! And I flew up and walked right inside. Yes! It was that big! And I looked around and God! It was beautiful! It was like this big, soft room . . . like a Bounce-A-Lot, only dewy. A big, huge, all-encompassing moist couch! But it was sweet, like, like, like a *huge peach pie* . . . only no crust. And I understood! I understood what you were telling me, Adria. You're so wise, so wise . . . "

Evan kissed me long and hard on the mouth, then got up and took a shower, leaving me to ponder his epiphany. What the fuck was he talking about? Not only is he a horrible lover, but now he's comparing my pussy to flourless pastry? And everyone knows that's not pie, that's melba!

After that Evan made an effort to please me every time, and it felt like an effort every time, like he was doing me this big favor. Like I was a little old lady and he was taking out my trash. Like it was this chore that he had to perform in order to, I don't know, get to visit the big pulsing vagina in his dreams. I kept thinking it would get better. He'd have another dream, another revelation. This time the vagina would give him his own vagina and make him figure it out or maybe she'd swallow him . . . although . . . then where would I be? Or maybe she could make him stop drinking so much and stop hanging out with dumb people. Maybe she could make love to him, I mean all of him, as though he was one big dick. I mean, he was, wasn't he? And then finally maybe he'd see. He'd walk out of the big, moist, peach moonwalk a new man, with a new, healthy, generous perspective on life and lovemaking. Or maybe if that didn't work, she could wrap her big, wet lips around him and squeeze the living shit out of him until he begged for mercy and promised to never, ever make another woman feel like her orgasm was a burden ever again.

I waited four more years for this revelation to come. I felt like she owed it to me, the big vagina in the sky. As a fellow sister, she needed to come through for me and deliver this message to Evan so that we could live happily ever after. Little did I know that the message had already been delivered . . . to me, not to Evan. It was my revelation, not his, and finally one day it hit me like a ton of bricks after his mother phoned to see if he was in, three weeks after he'd moved out.

With Evan, my vagina was a false hope, a pipe dream, a castle in the air—pleasant to contemplate, but very unlikely to be realized. Evan himself had told me as much . . . but I was too focused on not getting what I wanted to free myself.

After I told Evan's mother that he didn't live here anymore, I hung up the phone, turned on Wagner's *Lohengrin*, and made the best peach melba Brooklyn will ever know.

CHAPTER 4

MOB MENTALITY

people will do things in groups
they would never do alone

Otherwise known as "herd behavior," this term describes how a group of individuals can act without planned direction. It generally pertains to the behavior of animals in herds, flocks, and schools, and to human conduct during activities such as riots, sporting events, and Wal-Mart Black Fridays—often exhibiting increased aggression, violent behavior, and blind, animal instinct. When bedroom activity becomes a group activity, prepare for a sexual stampede in which the weakest are often trampled.

WHORE NEXT DOOR

by Whitney Cummings

When I was in college I lived in an apartment complex next door to a young couple. They were, like, late twenties, and I'd always hear them having crazy sex. It was loud and obnoxious, and I only masturbated to them a couple of times. For a while I actually thought the guy was beating her. Not that there's anything wrong with that. I don't judge. The way you discipline your girlfriend is your business. But it's, like, learn the value of a ball gag.

Then one night they randomly invited me to come to dinner with them. And so, like I do with everyone I despise, I went out with them.

Now this was before I had discovered Ativan, so the only remedy I had for social anxiety was drinking beverages such as Hennessy and amaretto sours; in this case a White Russian was also involved. Plus a bottle of wine. I basically opted to behave as if it were my final callback for *Flavor of Love*. So cut to me, shitfaced.

Now here's the thing: Most people slowly sober up. They gradually regain consciousness and awareness. Not me. I violently snap into sobriety—usually in the middle of some shameful and/or unhygienic act. So, this particular night, I go from ordering a delicious salad to having the guy's cock in my mouth and the girl's mouth on my cooter. I am smack in the middle of a threesome. To answer the implied question, no, I don't know if it was consensual. We can't even get into that minor point right now, because a stranger's cock is in my mouth.

I don't remember anything leading up to this point. I don't remember discussing the threesome, getting undressed, seeing the African art all over the walls.

I had never been in a threesome before, and I found it very complicated. There is a lot to juggle in a threesome: penis, balls, her vagina, her boobs, your boobs, your vagina, shame, avoiding genital warts. . . .

Couples who have threesomes have a system and a game plan; they do this all the time, but me, I'm just trying to pretend I know what I'm doing here and not use my teeth. I have big teeth, and when I have sex—be it with one *or* two people—all I think about is how to not impale my partner(s) with my incisors. Even when I masturbate, I worry that I may tooth myself to death.

So the next thing that happens is he unceremoniously removes his penis from my mouth—I would have liked to have had some say in that matter—and repositions himself to start having sex with his girlfriend from behind. Now she's eating me out and he's doing her from behind so her face is jamming into my cooter. Like, I'm getting fucked by her face. It feels, like, fine. I mean, it's a face. She is sort of mousy, so I don't feel much. It's not like she's Adrien Brody. Having sex with Adrien Brody's face would be a different story.

I don't know what to do with my hands, so I just do what every guy I've ever blown in the back of a car does. I place my hand on her head and do the "steering wheel" (how guys put their hands on the back of our heads and sort of tilt their heads and watch). I'm just trying not to make eye contact.

They both abruptly get up at the same time and thrust their respective genitals into my face. He puts his cock in my face, and she puts her vagina in my face. Which, by the way, is not shaved. Full bush. I'd always been a defender of the full bush, in support of feminism, but that was before I had to put my finger in one. Ladies: Clean it up. If you're going to date-rape your neighbor, the least you can do is trim the box. Don't be tacky.

So the girl takes my hand and guides me. Apparently, she wants me to finger her and jerk him off. Simultaneously.

Just as a side note: There is no music during this ordeal. In times like these you learn not to take music for granted. Can a girl get some *Now That's What I Call Music, Volume 17* or something? But here there is nothing to drown out the sounds of regret.

I try to find a rhythm of jerking him off and fingering her at the same time. It's basically an updated version of the head-pat/belly-rub. And I've never fingered a girl, so I'm just sort of aimlessly stabbing her uterus. It is so warm in there. I'm weirded out by it, so I behave like a *Fear Factor* contestant, wincing and grunting. Then they start making out above my head, so they close in on me and I have even less room to do my thing. And now my arms are getting tired, and hand jobs are already difficult because I never know what angle works. Like, for hand jobs I usually just use my vagina. So my arm muscles are burning.

But I'm not a quitter. My parents did not raise me to give up. So I work harder. Some crazy adrenaline kicks in, and in my mind I hear, Rudy! Rudy! Rudy! I just start milking like crazy and I hear him mumble something but I can't be stopped and then he ejaculates. Not on my face, but basically—it hits my shoulder and is in my hand.

I'm thinking, Nailed it. I just went from guest star to recurring, right? Wrong. The girl flips out. She starts yelling at him. She's pissed that he just did his thing. So she's screaming because I guess there is a rule between couples that you have to, like, finish with each other, not with the random neighbor. So they're literally naked fighting. She starts crying and I'm holding cum in my hand, which I promptly wipe on the couch. Then she starts yelling at me. She calls me a whore. I was like, "Me? A whore? Yeah, for sure." That's fair. It's sort of hard to defend your honor when you're holding jizz in your hand.

So I just get up and start gathering my stuff, which, by the way, is everywhere. Like, shirt in the bathroom, skort* in the kitchen. Some crazy shit unraveled before I fully sobered up. Like, it becomes blatantly clear to me later that I put up a fight. So I get my clothes and sneak out of there and into my apartment next door, where I have to awkwardly live next to them for the next two years.

Something I learned from this experience: Threesomes suck because you have to live with the fact that you gave *two* people herpes. And that two people don't call you back the next day.

THAT TIME I MOLESTED A GIRL
WHO HAD A MUSTACHE

by Jane Doe

It's the night of my friend Stacey's birthday party. Stacey and I are both cocktail waitresses at the same New York City bar, and despite the fact that several people have told me that she's in love with me, and despite the fact that on more than one occasion she's confessed that she can't stop "staring into my eyes," I think we're just gal pals.

I'm disappointed to see that our other coworker, Shoshanna Frank, who Stacey and I secretly call "Fronk," is also there. Fronk is a pear-shaped, bigger gal who wears loose-fitting Tibetan outfits, has wildly curly, unkempt hair . . . and a full mustache. Fronk is an angry wench of a waitress who is ten years our senior, smokes like a chimney, and never tips out the busboys. One doesn't have conversations with Fronk; one *listens* to her long monologues about her "work with Russian puppet theatre companies." I detest everything about Fronk.

So when the party comes to a close, I'm disappointed to realize that Fronk is one of the last women standing. I cannot bear another moment listening to the insane ramblings of Fronk. I try to lose her. At points I am blatantly rude to her. But Fronk will not go.

It's now five o'clock in the morning, and we're at my friend Mike's bar. I look over to see Fronk dancing a strange Indian dance around Stacey. I feel angry. I feel that Fronk is intruding on our good times. I. Hate. Fronk.

Then Fronk pulls out four tabs of ecstasy.

The events that proceed I'm not proud of. A half hour later, the ecstasy kicks in . . . and boy does it ever. Mike, Stacey, Fronk, and I end up at Mike's apartment. I become the leader of our high, making quick but thoughtful decisions. "We must all get in bed." As we walk over to the bed together, Stacey puts her hand on my back and tells me I'm doing a "great job." My eyes tear up and I say, "Thank you so much for recognizing me."

I begin directing our orgy. I tell Mike to kindly lie over there, I will be next to him, then Stacey, then Fronk. "Mike, we should start making out ASAP because I need to feel your beard on my face, and Stacey, if you would be so kind as to rub your tongue up and down the nape of my neck, that would be great." I want this to be a democratic, equal-opportunity orgy. As I wax poetic about my vision of our orgy, I realize: Mike is fingering me; Stacey is licking my nipples; I'm not touching anyone . . . but more importantly—where is Fronk?

Is that Fronk? No. Those are Mike's balls. Is that Fronk? No, that's Stacey's asshole.

Where, oh where is Fronk?

Finally I see her. Fronk is lying—facing away from the rest of us—curled up in the fetal position.

Hmph. I don't like *that*. I don't like that one bit.

Uh-oh. Fronk isn't cool with this. One of the players in our ensemble isn't committed. The imbalance of this energy is making me dizzy. Someone feels out of place. Someone feels not a part of things. A surge of purpose, singular and focused, runs through me. I stumble onto the floor and kneel before Fronk.

I move to softly kiss her lips. I see in her eyes what can only be described as naked fear. It's like making out with a piece of wood. I'm not sure if I hear the word "no." If I do, I ignore it.

I know one thing in this life. I must make sweet love to Fronk. I lick her earlobes, telling her she is "so beautiful."

"Oh, Fronk. My sweet Fronk."

PS: I'm so fucked up I don't realize I'm calling her "Fronk" to her face.

I try to pry her legs open, but she keeps clamping them shut. "You are a feisty little devil, Fronk!"

Suddenly, while kissing her hairy toes and saying to them, "I love you! Now I love you!" I feel Mike grab my shoulders and throw me back in the middle of a Stacey and Mike sandwich. They are jointly fingering me. Needless to say, I forget about Fronk.

But not for too long. I see Fronk on the edge of the bed in a thong, holding her stomach and calling a cab from her cell phone. *"Noooooooooooo!"* I yell. "Fronk can't go!" I jump over to her and wrap my arms around her like a monkey. Kissing her back acne. Softly. Tenderly.

"Fronk," I ask. "What can I do?" She shrugs her shoulders as if to say, "There's nothing."

Fuck this, I think. I look over and see Mike unsuccessfully trying to get Stacey to touch his penis. "Mike!" I say. "Get over here." Mike comes over and I see Fronk tense up, trying to hide her cellulite. Oh, I see. Of course. I'm such an idiot! I sit Mike in front of Fronk. And as though he's a marionette, I take his arms and close Fronk's eyes with his hands. Mike, via me, devours Fronk.

Every so often Mike tries to reach around to play with my boobs, but I slap his hands back into place where they rightly belong, around Fronk's ass. Soon enough Stacey jumps onto the Fronk train. I sit back, finally able to relax. And as I listen to sweet, gentle Fronk moan with pleasure, I think, Yes, my work here is done. I know success.

Then as the ecstasy starts to wear off I think, Fuck. I have a boyfriend.

CHAPTER 5

FOREIGN AFFAIRS

when bad sex goes abroad

Foreign travel involves many inherent dangers—language barriers, unexpected customs, obscure diseases—which you may come face-to-face with when getting frisky with a local. Herein are some tales of coital culture clash to keep tucked away in your fanny pack, along with some advice to bear in mind from the sexually well-traveled: Learn the basics of the native tongue: "yes," "no," "not on my face." Get vaccinated. Always know where your nearest exit is (keep in mind it may be behind you). Drink responsibly. And as a courtesy to fellow travelers, please be sure to stow all douchebaggage* before departure.

TRAPPED IN THE CLOSET

by "Suz"

Dear friends and family,

Greetings from Firenze! That's how they say "Florence" in Florence. We're finally here, and I've gotta say . . . London and Paris were *okay*, but now that we're in Italy I feel the trip is *really* starting. Peach orchards and olive groves; men in brown suits chasing beauties on bicycles; coin-tossed fountains and cobblestone cracks; and a freshly washed apron hanging from the window of our yellow hotel. Can you believe someone painted a building yellow? God, it's great to be twenty-two.

Tonight we're going to see the entire city of Florence by foot, on a pub crawl called the "Drunk Spaghetti Tour." Now, I know "pub crawl" sounds classless and juvenile, but remember—this is *Italy*. And a country that can turn the mundane into magic and romance *must* be able to redefine "trashy" and "intolerable," to stomp on those judgments like grapes until only the juice of whimsy remains.

I can't wait. We're meeting up with our guides on the steps of the Duomo at 1800 hours, and that's when the fun will begin. Ian, the lanky Danish intern, will hand us photocopied handwritten "coupons" that we'll redeem at each of the fourteen bars for free drinks, all of which have been ordered for us ahead of time and seem to be named after wrestling moves and abandoned porn titles. I will hop from one bar to another, making sure to absorb Old Europe's gentility while I down fluorescent purple shots with whipped cream on the rim.

After a while, Ian is going to start freestyle rapping in Danish. I know it doesn't sound like much from home, but believe me, when you're standing in the middle of a piazza, smelling leather markets and scooter exhaust, it's hard not to be turned on!

As half of you know, this has been a big year for me. I started hooking up with girls—which means two things: one, I *love* hooking up with girls; and two, I want desperately to not love hooking up with girls. You understand that my not-being-gay hinges only on finding the *right* guy. And here, on the Drunk Spaghetti Tour, I will convince myself that this guy is right in front of me. The shirtless one in the backpack. The one using his fluorescent purple mouth to freestyle rap in Danish.

I won't know what he's saying, but certain syllables will rhyme every time, and this will manage to impress me. He will improvise these complex rhymes quickly, and fluidly—it will never occur to me that he could just be spitting out memorized Danish hip-hop singles. How would I know? I don't listen to Hans Christian Anderseninem.

But that's when the magic will really kick in. Sitting on a pleather couch in a cramped and mirrored club—which, if it were in Wichita, would still be called a discotheque—Ian and I will begin our Roman holiday. A holiday of ouzo-laced kisses and public groping, which simply cannot be contained by a tiny divan in the corner of Shakira's grindy smoke trap.

So we will leave! We will jump on Ian's vespa and ride through the streets to some unknown corner of the city where no one will ever be able to find me—not even if I wanted or needed them to. He will take me to the pub crawl office—an abandoned closet in the middle of an alley, with nothing inside but a shelf full of flyers and a pair of dusty futon cushions. We will tear off our clothes and fall onto the cushions, kissing with the lust of emperors.

And then we will begin to have sex. Boy sex. Drunk boy sex. Drunk-with-a-stranger-who-is-no-longer-freestyle-rapping-in-Danish boy sex; on-the-cold-cement-floor-of-an-abandoned-closet boy sex; in-a-dank-and-moldy-alleyway, boy-in-my-alleyway sex. And that's when he'll notice that I am not enjoying this as much as other girls he's been with. That's when he'll stop . . . and say, so sweetly . . . "Have you been raped or something?" And because I won't have the heart to tell him no, because I don't want his feelings to be hurt by the fact that I haven't been raped, I will not give an answer. I will silently turn my head to the side and try to channel the slow, dramatic blink of Judith Light.

He'll leave in a hurry—not because of me, but because he has to go pick up his girlfriend from work. Boys!

Tomorrow we leave for Rome at 10 a.m. So exciting! But before we get to the train station, I have a *ton* of stuff to do. First I have to wake up naked in the crack between two futon cushions, realize where I am and what I've done and what that means about me as a person, get dressed, try to figure out what time it is, remember that I never told my friends last night that I was leaving, and get myself out of this closet!

Oh, but I won't be able to leave the closet, because it'll be locked from the outside. I know what you're thinking: Try to pick the lock with that broken red pen or the screw you found on the back of that waterless toilet—and, believe me, I will. I will fail at picking the lock, I will fail at prying the hinges off, I will fail at falling to my knees and clawing my way out of the closet with my fingertips. Eventually, I'll be crying so loudly that a delivery man will hear me as he parks his bike and show me the helpful European villager spirit by fiercely kicking the door in, allowing me to escape into the streets— mapless, compassless, friendless, moneyless—running like a rat through the Sunday-morning city with my bright white bra flapping behind me. Running over cobblestone cracks and empty gelato cups, past coin-tossed fountains, and chattering butchers, and old singing housewives, and ancient stone muses. Timeless, fearless, Italian.

Hope all is well in the Midwest,

Suz

THE FARTING RAPIST

by Alexandra Lydon

I fell in love when I was twelve years old. He was a petty Irish thief named Gerry.

I was watching the film *In the Name of the Father*. For those who don't know it, the film is set in Northern Ireland and London and involves the IRA, the British, and all hell breaking loose. But really everything I just mentioned means nothing without the man: Daniel Day-Lewis.

He wore tight corduroy pants, a beat-up red leather jacket, and had long greasy hair that he tucked behind his ears as he struggled to steal scrap metal off a rooftop, stopping only to play air guitar with a metal pole. He ran from the British and started a riot in the streets, throwing firebombs and bricks. He spoke in a thick Northern Irish accent, saying "*fook* dat," "for *fook's* sake," and "me dah was *fookin'* innocent." Needless to say, my twelve-year-old heart was *pounding*.

I directed my eyes to the sky in a dreamy adolescent way and thought, Someday I will meet my Northern Irish, possibly IRA-involved, greasy-haired man from the late eighties, early nineties.

Twelve years and so many Daniel Day's later, I found myself standing in a pub in Galway, Ireland. I was in the middle of a vacation with my friend Laura, the purpose of which was to get in touch with my "roots." Laura and I had been on a two-week-long hostel-hopping, culture-absorbing, pub-crawling Irish expedition. On this particular night she

had retreated to our hotel with a migraine, but I decided to
stay out, soak up the culture, and be among "my people."
The pub was packed, U2 was playing in the background, and
there was a sense of excitement in the air. It could have been
the four whiskeys I'd just inhaled, but there was something
different about this night. I could feel it.

And that's when it happened. That's when I saw him.

From across the room our eyes locked on each other. It
was my very own Daniel Day-Lewis look-alike, complete with
a red leather jacket, unnaturally tight pants, and long, dark
greasy hair. He stood casually against the wall, surrounded
by people, rolling a cigarette but never taking his eyes off
of me. Then suddenly as if walking out of my childhood, he
approached me and spoke.

"For fook's sake, what the fook are you doin' in a pub,
standin' around all by your fookin' self?"

Thank you.

The events that followed are fuzzy, but they involved
talking, laughing, and a lot of drinking. I heard his politi-
cal rants, primarily against the "British bastards," followed
by stories about growing up in Belfast amid the bombings
and the "Troubles." He told me his father was a general,
to which I replied, "Oh my God! My whole family is in law
enforcement! I come from a family of cops. That is such a
coincidence!"

He stopped. Stepped back and stared at me with a cold,
almost coy expression. He then slowly pressed his knuckles
into my skull as if holding a gun to my head and said, "I don't
like cops."

As I met his subtly threatening stare I realized the type of "general" he had been referring to and immediately thought, *Holy fook* . . . I am *really* turned on right now.

See, in that moment, with a virtual gun to my head, I realized that the universe had handed me the exact man I had asked for as a child. In that moment, I knew the true power of *The Secret*.

The transition from our meeting place to his apartment is hazy. I recall images of four or five different bar interiors, a creepy alley with a motorcycle chained to the wall that he claimed was his (but then couldn't seem to open the lock to), and the inside of a cab.

Eventually after a long ride, we were at his place, and he started to kiss me. The next transition is even more difficult to recall, but within fifteen seconds of the first kiss he had my pants and underwear off in one swift motion and was proceeding to mount me.

I lay motionless beneath him, trying to comprehend what was happening. As one eye stayed focused on him, the other began to peruse the wall next to me. It was littered with newspaper clippings of old IRA bombings delicately interspersed with posters of *Star Trek*.

I must pause here. It is important that I divulge a personal and somewhat repressed piece of my life. I was once on *Star Trek*. Not only was I on *Star Trek*, but I introduced a new "species" and I have a trading card. I now, five years later, can say with no regrets that I was a blind, telepathic Aenar from the Frost Vapor Lakes of the planet Andoria. I had an abnormally large forehead with a receding hairline.

I communicated through antennae. I rocked it. Now it's been said. I feel better. Not that this would really have mattered—especially because it is not as if he could have recognized me . . . or could he? Was I suddenly some weird Trekkie trophy fuck? Was I the blind Andorian to his Daniel Day?

I was immediately struck by a moment of sobriety. Potent clarity dawned on me. I've been through too much in my life. I am a smart person. It is time to stop doing stupid things. So I decided to stop the situation. First I tried the subtle and delicate approach: "I'm sorry, I can't do this, I just don't think this is right." Noticing this was not working, I transitioned to the more aggressive approach of: *"Get the fuck off me right now!"* When even that method didn't work, a rather awkward struggle ensued until I somehow managed to push him off me and to the other side of the bed, where he accepted defeat by instantly falling asleep.

Okay.

I lay there, covering myself with a sheet printed with *South Park* characters, and the panic and disgust began to grow from within.

Now I need to make one thing clear. I understand that after one is almost raped, one should probably . . . leave. I fully encourage this, and under most circumstances I would have done so; however, in this case I was in a foreign country, I had no idea where I was, it was the middle of the night, I had spent all my cash, and as a former Girl Scout I can recite in the handbook where it says, " 'tis better to deal with danger in daylight than in darkness."

So I stayed. I stayed and became a prisoner in a foreigner's bedroom. Come to think of it, it actually kind of looked like a cell. A cell with *South Park* sheets. My own personal nightmare. As I lay there silent and still, hoping that he wouldn't wake up and praying for a glimpse of sunlight to come through the window, signaling it was safe for me to flee, I heard the prophetic words of Gerry's father after he and Gerry were wrongfully imprisoned for a crime they didn't commit.

I saw the scene so clearly in front of me. A tired and sick man who was still so full of faith faced me. He pointed at his head and said, "All they done was block out the light. They can't block out the light in here."

He was right. The only way I was going to make it till dawn was to use my mind to take me away. So I remained perfectly still and did the only rational thing I could think to do: visualization exercises. Breathing in yellow light, breathing out fear and disgust. Breathing in protective light, breathing out unsuccessful rapist lying next to me. Just as I began to feel myself relax and allow myself to be absorbed by yellow light, it happened. . . .

He farted.

It was the loudest release of gas I have ever heard in my entire life. This was no ordinary passage of wind. There is no real way to describe it, other than that it sounded like a foghorn. It wasn't quick either. It was long. It was a long, *power-ful* foghorn, and it actually shook the bed. And me as well—it shook me. It shook me to the core.

I tensed up, not knowing what to expect. I thought, Surely

the beast has been awakened by his own fart. But nothing; he didn't even stir.

Then it happened again. And again. He proceeded to fart every two minutes for the next hour. Each fart had its own quirky personality. One came with such force that it actually lifted him from the bed. One had such a deep, bellowing nature that I feared the mighty cliffs of Ireland may have crumbled where they stood.

I rolled to the very edge of the bed and curled into a ball, trying to comfort myself while simultaneously creating a small target. I envisioned pink lavender being wrapped around me like a ribbon. A ribbon of protection. A bubble of love. But nothing could protect me. They just kept coming.

I directed my eyes back up to the sky and asked, "Really? Is this what I get? *Really?*"

Finally, as light began to fill the room, my eyes burning with grief, I quietly reached for my purse. He stirred!

I thought, You're waking up now?

Before he could speak, I blurted out, "I need a cab!" At which point he sat up, turned up the volume on his TV, and said, "Well, *Star Trek* comes on in two minutes. I'll walk you down after that."

"That's okay," I said with a forced grin. "I'll find it."

He called after me, but I didn't look back. I kept moving. I burst through one door, then another, finally making it out onto the street. The cold rain hit my face, and a surge of gratitude for my life and freedom came over me. As I stood alone in the rain on the streets of the Irish ghetto, I felt

reborn . . . and extremely hungover. In that moment I realized two things: One, I had no idea where or what the name
of my hotel was. And two, my Daniel Day-Lewis was a flatulent Trekkie.

I made it back to my hotel, after a taxi driver found me
wandering aimlessly down the street. I described what my
hotel looked like and explained with tears running down
my face that I had no money to pay him. A kind Irish cabbie, he drove me there anyway. When I arrived back to my
hotel I found Laura finishing her sixth shower of the evening/morning. We both sat there, me in my clothes from the
night before describing in detail the battle I had just been
through, her with a towel on her head, hands pruned from
the number of showers she had taken to stave off the anxiety of thinking I was dead. And then for a while we didn't
say a word.

The next words spoken were from Laura's mouth. "We
will call him the 'Farting Rapist,'" she said.

Yes, we will.

Addendum: A few months ago the Farting Rapist
(we'll call him "Roy") sent me a Facebook friend request
with a message attached that read, "Hola, muchacha . . .
Remember me?" I nearly fell off my chair; it had been
almost two years since I had seen that greasy hair and
subtly threatening smile. There he was, staring back at
me in a trying-to-be-casually-good-looking, unsuccessfully-tried-to-crop-out-the-person-standing-next-to-him
Facebook profile pic, and I felt ill. I wanted to respond to

him, "I do remember you, 'Roymond.' There are things in life you never forget, like being fart raped by an assumed member of the IRA."

Instead I hit "Ignore" and went back to spying on people from high school whom I hated.

AN AMERICAN ALCOHOLIC IN LONDON

by Rachel F.

At the end of the twentieth century I attended a private university in upstate New York, to which my parents contributed a few thousand dollars per month so that I could, on the occasion of, let's say, "morning," roll over to one side of my bed, take hits from a very expensive glass bong, and choose not to attend a class called "Stars, Galaxies, and the Universe," which I took pass/fail. After two years of this routine, things had gotten a bit stale, and I decided I was due for a change of scenery. I signed up for the "junior year abroad." I chose London because a language barrier seemed strenuous.

I was twenty at the time, ripe and ready. I joined my fifty closest college friends on a jet plane one January evening and headed for my well-funded European vacation. I waited, with bated breath, for the moment when we were high enough in the sky where the legal drinking age of the United States of America disappeared . . . when I would be free.

We all drank Bloody Marys after we reached cruising altitude. We looked at each other between the cracks of the seats and announced to what degree we were "wasted." We passed out; we woke up; we continued drinking. This wasn't the first time we had gotten drunk, but it was the first time we were drunk on a plane heading toward six months in a foreign land on our parents' dime under the guise of a meaningful cultural learning experience. It was special.

Upon our arrival in customs, I slurred my words while trying to explain to the immigration officer the work permit I needed for my fancy internship. The immigration officer, potentially post-early-morning pint, slurred right back to me, "Welcome home." I couldn't tell if this was some kind of signal from the universe or if he was just bleary-eyed and wasn't paying attention to the navy blue sheen of my American passport. Regardless, it was profound.

The thing was, London instantly *felt* like home to me. Finally, I was living in a land where it was socially acceptable to drink alcohol all day long. The British were like family. Back stateside, all I had ever been told about *my* family was that Jews don't drink. As you could imagine, based on my aforementioned behavior, this baffled me.

I shared a flat in central London near Notting Hill with two other twenty-year-old women who silently hated each other and one obsessive-compulsive man. It was rough in there, but we found a way to coexist with the help of cheap red wine and hashish, which was readily available via a fifteen-year-old Pakistani boy I'd befriended named Abdul, whom we called "Abs" for short.

On the weekends we traveled to mysterious European cities where we could obliterate ourselves while people spoke a different language. Because I had honed the skill in London, it became my self-appointed responsibility to procure the drugs when we arrived at each port. Every assignment involved a dark and more-than-slightly frightening scenario with a man of European descent pressed up against me—reeking of booze and Drakkar Noir—with his tongue in my mouth and his fingers inside my pants. I was successful in scoring drugs for my crew on every occasion and chalked up the finger bangs to "getting to know the locals."

Back in London at the fancy internship, my boss's name was Lucy. She was raised in the midlands of England and was "li-tra-lee" *incomprehensible* for the first two weeks I worked for her. I feared for my tenure with her until one night after a press opening of a Stephen Sondheim revival, I discovered she enjoyed drinking and passing out in banquettes as much as I did. Lucy was a self-made woman; she'd risen to a prominent rank in the British social class and had a membership at a private club in Soho that came with an account to which she could charge drinks. Lucy would take me there after a long day of work because she knew I'd put her in a cab when the number of vodka gimlets she'd drunk through a straw had impaired her ability to see.

One night, with a shoulder damp with tears and other facial secretions, after Lucy sobbed and professed her *true* and *genuine* love for me, stating I was the best intern she'd ever had, I made an executive decision to send her home. Before heading to the Tube, I gave her account number a whirl and ordered myself a drink.

I wasn't alone at the bar for very long. I was dressed in a fashion that said "slutty bougie hippie." I wore five-inch red-leather platform boots, long beaded necklaces that hung below my belly button, and a formfitting backless dress with a plunging neckline. As it turns out, barely legal American college girls in revealing costumes are *indeed* intriguing to wealthy British dudes who belong to private clubs. I made small talk with one such gentleman who sidled up to me at the bar. I made eye contact and pretended to know about British politics. After many nights abroad talking to all sorts of European fellows who leered at me and paid for my drinks, I had cultivated this skill of saying "exactly" at just the right moment and could fool most into thinking that I actually knew something. I knew nothing. All I really and truly knew was that the song "One More Time" by Daft Punk felt like my personal anthem. So when the DJ played it in the midst of that particular conversation, I abandoned the man and spun into the area in the lounge that the patrons had turned into an impromptu dance party.

There were a dozen or so British people who must have felt the same about the song as I did, and we smooshed together on the spot that we'd turned into a dance floor. It was hot and sweaty, and you could really feel that something was happening. And then something really happened. Midsong, I jumped as high as I could in my boots, and midair, I felt a strong arm grab me around the waist and pull me down. It belonged to a man. He was wearing a tuxedo and had floppy dark hair. He was smiling and looking at my face and holding my twenty-year-old body tightly in one arm while clutching a bottle of champagne with his free hand. He took a swig of the champagne from the bottle, then offered me some. In the memory—or my fantasy—he spun me away from him, then pulled me back into him and dipped my entire body until it was inches from the floor. Daft Punk was still blasting, and I was transfixed by the tuxedoed gentleman and his moves. He held me with his bottle of champagne against his chest.

He looked deeply into my eyes, breathed heavily against my neck, and whispered into my ear. He asked me if I cared to join him in the loo. I took this to mean cocaine, because that's what it always meant. I nodded slowly, looking at his sweaty face, and then definitively and breathlessly exclaimed, "I'd love to join you in the loo."

I remember the walk down the stairs. I remember the stall of the men's bathroom that we both entered. I remember the ripping off of a bow tie. I remember the tossing off of the tuxedo jacket, and I remember a tugging of his suspenders. I *vaguely recall* the moment he told me I was "naughty for not wearing knickers." I *cannot forget* him lifting me, placing me in a standing position on top of the toilet seat, clad only in my boots and dangling beaded necklaces, where I stood, legs spread open, hands clutching either side of the stall, as he performed *artful* cunnilingus upon me from below.

I remember looking down, bewildered, at the man in the patent leather shoes and suspenders who was eating my pussy, and then, I remember the banging.

The banging is quite clear in my mind. I do not mean "banging" in a metaphorical sense—I mean the literal pounding of fists on the bathroom door. I cannot erase the memory of the large British bouncer glaring at me, as I stood there on the toilet seat, clad only in red-leather platform boots and my long hippie necklaces. The bouncer, accompanied by an equally large and intimidating companion, screamed, *"See that girl, see that guy—don't ever let them in here again!"* Then he bellowed that the club closed hours ago, and we needed to put our bloody clothes on. It was dramatic, I think.

I'm pretty sure it was humiliating. It's hard to deny it was shameful. Then the bouncer kicked us out of the club.

After we were left alone on the street, the man told me I had a beautiful vagina and that he had to get up early in the morning for work . . . and then disappeared into the night. My banishment from the club coincided with the end of my junior year abroad, so there weren't any awkward moments with Lucy. My European education ended with a bang.

My junior year abroad remains a profound cultural experience, even with the fingers, the tongues, the drugs, and the drinks. I wish I could tell you I never did anything like this again, that this was the moment I hit bottom. But there was more research to be done, in a multitude of cities, with other concoctions, dance moves, and dudes I barely knew. Because as it turns out, *Jews do drink*, and sometimes they drink too much.

After about fifty more finger bangs with strangers whilst under the influence, I decided to throw in the towel. I'm happy to report that today I do things differently. I no longer drink or do drugs; when traveling or here at home, I get to know the locals by eating their food, drinking their coffee, smoking their cigarettes, and *talking* to them.

A WILDE NIGHT IN PARIS

by Jackie Clarke

On the night before I was to leave Paris, my dream of a tor-rid European love affair had still been unrealized. In fact, the closest I had gotten to sex was when my father pointed out a whorehouse that his morbidly obese friend, Marvin Denard, frequented.

My sex life up until this point was decidedly less romantic than what cable television had promised. Romance didn't exist at my college in New Hampshire. Sure, getting it doggy style on a bare twin mattress can be fun, but I was in Paris and I wanted more. I thought it was time to finally have the passion I craved. My Parisian lover would pour champagne and read me poetry. We'd take a bath together while he fed me strawberries. He would never ask for a blowjob while he played video games.

Being on a family vacation was an obstacle to my goal. Aside from days filled with group activities, there was also the fact that I was sharing a room with my brother. Another, perhaps bigger obstacle was my profound lack of personal style. The women of Paris wear chic scarves and high heels. I dressed for comfort, favoring baggy jeans, sweatshirts, and cotton underwear purchased at CVS. My makeup was ChapStick. My moisturizer was Vaseline. I hadn't discovered eyebrow waxing or, to be honest, any sort of waxing. My pubic area looked like Robin Williams's chest.

On that last day of my trip, my parents and brother took the train to Versailles while I visited the Père Lachaise cemetery. The overcast skies fit my mood as I walked through the old graveyard in search of the final resting places of Isadora Duncan and Marcel Marceau. The tomb of Abelard and Héloïse, monument to one of history's juiciest love affairs, silently mocked me. Abelard was a teacher and Héloïse was a nun and *they* managed to get it on. When I stopped at Oscar Wilde's gravestone—a bizarre stone angel with a broken and missing penis—I saw it as a symbol of my failure. It wasn't fair. I was twenty-one and in Paris. Why couldn't I have an affair?

That night my parents and brother headed to bed early in order to be fresh for the plane the next morning. I decided if I couldn't have an affair I was going to do the next best thing: get drunk. So I put on a pair of jeans and my favorite shapeless Guatemalan sweater, the kind that always have wood chips buried deep in the fabric, and headed downstairs.

The hotel bar was empty except for a young English couple who struck up a conversation with me. They bought bottle after bottle of wine, and we drank and laughed well into the evening. It was turning into a sublime last night in Paris, and would have been had I just left it at that. But then the American businessman walked in. From the moment he plopped down beside me and flashed me his red wine–stained smile, I knew this man would be mine. He was not the dark-haired Parisian lothario I had fantasized about, but it was one in the morning and I was desperate.

The English couple headed off to bed soon after he joined us. I imagine it was the businessman's habit of shouting instead of speaking that drove them away. I didn't mind, as

I was now alone with my soon-to-be conquest. The business-man informed me, in his flat midwestern accent, that his consulting firm had sent him to Paris for a week. He had a face that looked like a baby's, if left out in the sun for too long—a less attractive Ted Kennedy with a bright red, veiny nose and a gut stretching his blue oxford shirt almost to the breaking point. He was older. Probably older than my father. Embarrassing as it is to think back on it now, I was very excited to be with this stranger whose mouth bubbled up in the corners with little blobs of spittle every time he spoke.

I started to flirt, which was not something I was skilled at. In the fifth grade, I let Eddie Llamar know I liked him by asking him to kiss my foot, then kicking him in the face. With the businessman I took a less aggressive approach. I told him I was an Aquarius, and he told me he was a Leo. I jokingly asked if that meant he was a lion. He burst into laughter, which quickly dissolved into violent coughing. All the while I maintained an awkward smile and sipped my wine. This man would have to drop dead at my feet to prevent me from achieving my goal. I was going to have an affair.

When I suggested we head upstairs to his room, he looked like I had offered him free cable television for life. He nearly fell as he stumbled to his feet. I grabbed his liver-spotted hand and led him out of the bar. We got to his room and he closed the door. It was really happening. I was so excited that I actually felt taller. He pulled me close and kissed me. I could feel his soft body pressed against mine. His kissing technique was peculiar. His mouth had a narrow range of motion, as if it only opened wide enough to accommodate a large grape.

He patted at my breasts the way a large child, unaware of his own strength, pats a dog. Then he threw me on the bed. And by "threw" I mean he unathletically motioned for me to get on the bed. I felt like I was being seduced by a less sexually vibrant Santa Claus. He pulled my jeans off, then slid my CVS underwear down my unshaven legs. And he went down on me.

Now, any man who goes straight for the lady-goods gets an *A* for effort in my book. It's usually a sign of good character, a man who's been raised well. But something was wrong. The businessman's tongue was cold. It was the oddest thing. It was like I was being eaten out by a sentient corpse. It was profoundly unsexy. I closed my eyes and prayed for his tongue to warm up. It didn't. I tried to feign pleasure and started bucking my hips in the hope that he would fall off me. But the businessman's tongue stayed in the saddle. I couldn't pretend any longer. I would have a better chance at an orgasm if I pressed a raw chicken cutlet square against my vagina. I had to admit the truth: Things were not going well with the affair.

I pushed his head away midcunnilingus and began to dress. The businessman sat up and asked me what I was doing. I turned and looked at his sad, round, wet face and told him, "I can't do this." And I left.

When I think back on the events of that night, I think of the old adage, "Be careful what you wish for." Or as Oscar Wilde once wrote, "When the gods wish to punish us, they answer our prayers." Amen to that.

CHAPTER 6

THE SIZE AND SHAPE OF THINGS

some of life's harder anatomy lessons

A timeless question: Does size really matter?
A timeless answer: Yes.

The human body comes in all shapes and sizes, sometimes with a few . . . surprises. Our aim is not to be shallow. We believe that all of God's creatures are beautiful. Who's to say what "normal" is . . . right? Actually, there are occasions when it is okay—no—necessary to stand up and say, "That is not normal." The following contributors will attempt to do just that in these stories. Because apparently they were not brave enough to do it in the moment. And let's be honest, neither would we.

FATTY AND THE FAKE DICK

by Dorien Davies

My quarter-life crisis involved a lot of cake. As the proud recipient of a bachelor's of fine arts, my post-college day job was neither artistic nor fine. It did, however, include a great deal of frosting. This is because I spent my days working at a four-star hotel as a banquet server. I waited on hoards of rich, Persian, Jewish thirteen-year-olds at their opulent bar/bat mitzvahs. I kid you not, one of their mothers had the Star of the Sea pendant from *Titanic* on her neck. The *real* one. I also served soon-to-be-rich, white, blonde twenty-somethings at the receptions of their weddings to cheesy, Hollywood-type grooms twice their ages. Whenever I realized what I had done with my life and my parents' hard-earned tuition, or if the tiniest trace of existentialism graced my mind, I remedied the situation by leaving work with a pound and a half of leftover Sweet Lady Jane wedding cake, eating the whole thing by myself, and crying until my cat sat on my face to shut me up.

After two years of said behavior, I had gained a total of forty-five pounds. I lost my waist, my boobs turned into saggy, fat sacks, and my arms became leglike. You might say I didn't gain weight well—it sort of went everywhere. I wasn't curvy or voluptuous—no—more like a sausage. I respect women of all shapes and sizes, but since it was me and I was in a period of self-loathing, I began to refer to myself as "Fatty." I *know*.

I was chronically lonely. And I did everything in my power to try to hide my new body. It's funny how fatties try to conceal their fatty: I applied a lot of fake tanner; I abused eye makeup; I showed more cleavage—hoping these measures would draw attention away from the rest of the fiasco. In hindsight, I just ended up looking like a slutty, orange fatty who probably worked at MAC.

I stayed single for two years, watching other people get married several times weekly. And I became hungry for men like I had never been hungry before, not even for cake. Then one day, Cade moved into my complex.

The first time I saw him he pulled into the driveway in a brand-new Mercedes: silver, unusual. He stepped out of the car like a man coming home from a long day of fighting crime or putting out fires while teaching orphans to fish. He looked like an Abercrombie model—except without the cowboy hat and inherent air of gay. I watched him unload his car in the hot weather, and when he took off his shirt, I put down my cake, staring out my bedroom window like Emily Dickinson. For months, I watched him, my voyeurism satiating my loneliness as well as my need for cake.

Cade was popular and had lots of "friends." They drove fancy cars and would show up in the middle of the day. They'd stay for an hour or so and then leave with some kind of gift bag. My neighbor was so generous.

He dated beautiful girls. I say "girls" because I'm pretty sure most of them were underage. Sometimes I could hear him having sex with them because his bedroom was directly under mine, and teenagers are always screamers. I thought it intriguing and eccentric that he liked young girls. Not statutory rape at all.

We finally ran into each other at the mailbox one morning. At first I was confused because when he spoke to me I didn't understand what he was saying. I thought he had an accent or something. But then I realized, no, he was just very, *very* dumb. In fact, I had never met a man so dumb. But so very *very* hot that the dumb didn't much matter to me at all. I think Cade could sense my desperation, because a few days later he came up the stairs and knocked on my door.

"Hi, d'you wanna see my 'partment and smoke a joint?" he said, sounding like Rocky Balboa if he had a broken jaw and an anesthetized tongue.

"Well, if you put it that way," I said, "yes!"

His apartment was dark. There was a turgid brown leather couch under a drawn curtain, a huge flat-screen television and twenty-five two-quart jars of weed sitting on his counter. The most noticeable thing, however, was the overwhelming stench. It was like someone had taken a bottle of skunk spray, basil, and Taco Bell, spilled it inside a parked car on a hot day, and then made me sit inside it. I looked around and then looked at him and said, "It's so nice in here."

"Thanks," he said (almost incomprehensibly). "So you smoke?"

"Um . . . sure," I said, hoping I had answered the right question.

"These are just samples," he said, gesturing to the jars on the table.

Now at this point all I heard was mumbling. I was totally checked out, just standing there hoping that he wouldn't fall into some kind of seizure before we could make out at least a little. Then he said, as clear as day, "I've got a lot more weed over here," and gestured to the ceiling-high pile of moving boxes in the corner. Yeah, that's right, people—what amounted to probably five hundred pounds of weed. That's a lot of felonies.

"Oh," I said, "is this what you do?"

"Yeah," he perked up. "I mean, I used to be a commercial agent, but the strike put me out of business."

He pulled out a joint and handed it to me with a lighter that said "The Standard." I thought it ironic since I had just lost all of mine. We sat down and smoked while he turned on the Christian Broadcasting Network. We didn't speak another word until the joint was out, then he turned to me and said, "Jesus has some good lessons," and in the same moment kissed me. I was crazy stoned; my mouth felt like powder. His mouth tasted like burnt nasty. But within seconds my pants were off my body, like a sausage out of its casing.

I was having so much fun. Our two bodies collided in a fury of pent-up sexual tension, with a fifty-inch plasma screen image of Jesus of Nazareth watching over us. It was glorious.

And then I put my hand in Cade's boxers. I remember thinking, "This can't be right. No, no, this is wrong. Danger. Danger." You see, the head of Dummy's penis was the size of a baseball. Literally, a baseball. It was a freakish, fleshy orb, and I did not know what the hell to do with it. At any other time in my life I would have recoiled, put on my pants, gone home, and ordered pizza. But I was naked with the man that I had been stalking for months. Naked with someone for the first time in the better part of a year. And even though I was high out of my mind, and I was sure that I was shrinking and I could see magical dancing rainbows all around me, I had already made so many concessions to get to this point, what was one more? Fuck it. I could take it. Even if it tore me apart. I'm a real woman and I have needs.

And so it was. And it *was* big. And it felt very, very uncomfortable. But it was sex! And I was back! I was golden again! I felt beautiful and sexy and perfect and then . . .

I looked down and I saw the orange dimples in my thighs being exaggerated by the glow of Jesus on the TV and the friction of Dummy's body weight. It looked nasty, like macaroni and cheese, and it tore me out of my joy. I suddenly became horribly self-conscious. I looked up at him to see if he had seen it too, but he hadn't. No, he hadn't . . . because he was watching television.

He saw me looking up at him, but instead of apologizing he pulled out his freakish penis head, pulled off the condom (which fit surprisingly well) and asked me to finish him off with my mouth. Because he said he "couldn't really feel anything anyway." Or at least I think that's what he said. I was mortified, but I did it anyway. Why? Because I was way too invested, that's why. Now, as I approached his penis and saw it up close for the first time, I noticed something strange, something unnatural. I found a distinctive hard ridge around the bottom of the head, almost like a bone, which moved under the skin when you touched it . . . and just beneath it was a small scar. It was like a cartilage implant. An implant. In his penis. A penis implant. In his penis. Cade's big ole, nasty, freakish, fleshy cock head was fake? Who does that? I had finally had enough. After the blowjob, I went home. (Yes, I finished him off, but it was only out of sheer curiosity.) Then I had a piece of cake and fell asleep. And I slept like a baby.

The next morning, I walked over to his apartment and did one of these: "Are we cool? 'Cause that was not what I really intended on doing. I was stoned, don't know why that happened . . . I mean, we're neighbors . . . and I'm not really interested in you at all." I think he grunted a response and then that was it.

I went back upstairs and closed the curtains and tried to surmise how I had gotten into this situation in the first place, and how to keep myself from getting there ever again. Why had I been so desperate? Why had I let all of my standards go just to keep from being alone? This Fatty-phase wasn't forever. I could change. My situation was temporary. His was not. I mean, I may have been a fatty, orange waitress, but he was a dumb, rude, Jesus freak, drug-dealing pedophile with a massive enunciation problem and a desensitized penile implant. Surely a vibrator is better than that.

Two months later, the police raided his apartment. And that night, I sat on my toilet, applying my self-tanner and listening to the chaos below me, and I wondered how jail would treat Cade. Would the inmates be as illuminated by his flaws as I was? I hoped so. Because, you know, they don't have cake in jail.

THE "M" WORD

by John Flynn

It's a wintry February afternoon in 2007, and I find myself in an all too familiar situation: bored, horny, and alone. And high. And for once, getting high just isn't enough. Rather than wallow in my own misery, I decide to take a look at Craigslist. This is an activity I rarely resort to and never undertake with any sense of pride. I view online hookups as fast food: They're cheap, easy, and rarely satisfying, but sometimes it's all you want and the only thing you can emotionally afford.

So I'm poking around the M4M Casual Encounters section, and eventually I find an ad that seems like a safe bet. I e-mail the guy, he e-mails me back, and soon we're chatting over IM. Everything is looking good: He lives nearby, he has an okay-looking face (meaning he's not totally attractive, but a good personality will make up for it), he wants me to do to him what I feel like doing to someone, and he has his own place. I get dressed in my nicest and most easily removable winter outfit, and start getting ready to seize my Sunday afternoon. I'm about to leave when he hits me with one final IM.

"Oh, I should probably tell you, I'm a little person."

The word "little" confuses my cloudy mind-set, and I write back, "Do you mean you're very petty?"

"No," he replies. "I'm three feet four inches tall."

Now I happen to clock in at six foot two, so that's half my height (in stoner math). And at first I feel betrayed. This is clearly a case of withholding vital information. Information that you know will affect whether or not people will respond to your ad. I begin to wonder how I can bow out of this gracefully.

But before I respond, he adds, "If you don't want to come over, I understand."

And immediately I feel like an asshole. It occurs to me that this poor guy probably has such a difficult time meeting someone, even on the cyber cathouse I call Craigslist, that if he is upfront about his size, then he either doesn't get any responses, or only gets them from fetishists. And that probably makes him feel even more objectified and less like a real person than your average Craigslist encounter.

My tall man guilt takes over, and I tell myself that I can be the bigger man—I mean I can rise above the situa—I can soldier through. Who knows, I might even like it. I never thought I'd like an Adam Sandler movie, but *You Don't Mess with the Zohan* proved me wrong. Maybe this guy was the Zohan of little people?

"No problem!!!" I try to write back as enthusiastically and with as many exclamation points as possible. "See you in a few!!!!"

"Great," he responds, so I smoke another bowl, and head out to meet a very different destiny than the one I had gone looking for.

As I make my way over to his place, I create a list of rules for myself. No double takes. React to everything that happens as if it's totally normal. And under no circumstances are you to use the "m" word. They find it incredibly insulting! By the time I arrive, I feel like I have a solid game plan, and I've almost convinced myself that this will be fun. After all, I am about to have some no-strings-attached sex, and that's what I originally went looking for.

I get to his apartment and ring the bell. The door opens, and standing there is a fully grown man who comes up to my waist. Luckily I'm already so stoned that it would take too long for me to do a double take.

He says in a thick southern twang, "Hey, nice to meet you. Come on in."

"Thanks," I reply. "Where do you come from with that bewitching accent?"

"Just outside of Georgia," he says, and then adds coquettishly, "Can you tell?"

I smile at his old-school flirting and think this might not be as bad as I feared. As we walk in he adds, "Sorry about the mess, I had a show last night."

"Oh, what do you do?"

"I perform with a drag troupe all over the city as Mini-Minnie Pearl."

Wow, I think to myself, a midget drag queen from the South. How rare is that? It's like I'm about to fuck a unicorn. Then I immediately chide myself for just *thinking* the "m" word.

We walk into his living room and he turns to me and says, "Would you like to get high?" I do my best to stifle a stoner giggle fit as I think to myself, A little person just asked me to get high! But I recover quickly and say "sure" as I take a seat on his sofa. I am already high as can be, but I know that it's impossible for me to be *too* stoned for this experience. He starts to pack a bowl, but his hand is shaking while he does it. Before I can ask about it, he says, "Don't worry about this, it happens all the time."

"No problem," I say out loud as I quietly think to myself, I guess if someone twice my size was about to fuck me, I'd be a little shaky too.

So we smoke a bit and start chatting about movies we've recently seen, the weather, the quality of the weed we're smoking—the usual stuff you want to get out of the way before you bone a complete stranger. Besides, I figure if I know the name of his drag persona we're not exactly strangers. Once we're done smoking, he puts the bowl down, and then he jumps on my lap and we start making out.

Now, I'm totally used to having dudes on my lap. But I'm used to having more dude on my lap than what I'm getting. I'm trying to act like this is all normal, but it's disconcerting to be able to hold the entire ass of an adult man in just one of your hands.

Our make-out session progresses, and I find myself closing my eyes and pretending I'm making out with someone else. Unfortunately each fantasy only lasts for a few seconds. This is partially because I am so blitzed by this point that I can't keep a train of thought for long. But mainly it's because my partner loves to talk dirty in his thick southern drawl, which makes him sound like a pornographic Paula Deen. So our making out is punctuated with such gems as, "Yeah, that's what I'm talkin' 'bout!" "Damn, you kiss so sweet," and "Yeah baby, give Daddy your sugar!" I don't know what gives him the idea that he's the "daddy" in the situation, and I'm annoyed that I have to constantly reboot my imagination and come up with another pretend lover to make out with.

I have no desire for this to last any longer than it needs to, so I get our clothes off as quickly as possible, until eventually we're both standing naked in front of each other. He stares at me, eye level to my junk, as he says, "Ooh, I love me a good fire crotch." (Yes, I'm a redhead.)

Then he goes up on me.

After a few minutes of this it's time to take this beyond the couch level and start the main event. I know this because my host looks up and into my eyes and says, "Are you ready to take the ride of your life?" All I can do is shrug as he takes me by the hand and leads me to his bedroom.

The bed is a typical queen-size bed. However, at the end of the bed there is a set of those doggie steps that people use for their pets. He scampers up them to the bed as fast as possible and lands in what he thinks is a seductive pose: one arm holding up his head and the other one resting alluringly on his hip. He looks like a horizontal half-pint Mae West. I am too stoned not to appear shocked by this. And immediately I feel guilty for not hiding my shock better, as clearly no one wants to be seen using anything that's meant for pets. In retrospect I should have used them too and said something like, "Oh, thank God! Someone *else* uses these things!"

Just as I'm about to join him on the bed, the phone on his bedside table rings. He looks at the caller ID and says, "Oh, hold on, I have to take this." Then he grabs the phone, hops off the bed, and goes out in the hallway to talk. And immediately my trepidation turns to indignation. I mean, hello!

We're in the middle of something that I don't even really want to be a part of, and you choose to take a phone call when I am standing naked in front of you? I am so insulted that without thinking I say, "Midget! Midget! Midget!" in a loud whisper.

I regain my composure soon enough and try to figure out a way to take advantage of this turn of events. I'm racking my brain, but nothing useful is coming to me. Turns out I was wrong earlier; I actually am too high to deal with this situation. As I look around his room, all I see are small piles of sequins and wigs and small heels. Now I'm even more disgusted that this drag queen doesn't care enough to treat his outfits with any respect. What does that say about his commitment to the craft?

A few minutes have gone by when my host comes back into the room and says, "I'm really sorry, but that was my wife. And she's on her way over with my son, and they'll be here in fifteen minutes, so you have to leave."

A tidal wave of relief washes over me, and without another word I return to the living room to get my clothes. The poor little guy must be mistaking my enthusiasm for disappointment because while I'm getting dressed he's very apologetic. Clearly he's embarrassed, but his southern upbringing trained him to be gentlemanly about the situation. It also trained him that it's cool to have sex with dudes on Craigslist while being married with kids, but that's the South for you.

As I walk to the door, I tell him not to worry, that these things happen, and it's not a big deal. And soon enough I am on my way out.

"I just feel terrible," he says to me at the door. "I really wanted to give you an afternoon you'd never forget."

"Then don't worry," I reply. "That's exactly what you did."

THE WAY-TOO-PERSONAL ASSISTANT
by Emmy Rowland

Los Angeles is the land of opportunity, and I have had many glamorous jobs since moving here. Among them are: dog walker, nanny, receptionist at an EZLube, and construction worker. I had the pleasure of hanging three hundred door-knobs in a hotel—oh, now that was fun. I was the only girl. I wore overalls to really look the part but was told later that I put half the doorknobs on backward. Yeah, so I smoked weed in my car instead of eating lunch everyday. Backward is a matter of opinion. They were only *backward* if you were going *out* the door. And as if these jobs didn't build my self-esteem enough, I became a personal assistant to some of LA's rich and famous.

Like all personal assistants of drunk, drug-addicted, nar-cissistic actresses, I was treated with the utmost respect. For the sake of this story we'll call her "Shana." It seems suf-ficiently snobby. Shana was beautiful, I mean, otherworldly beautiful. She was a former international model turned actress. Even after all-nighters, I never saw this woman look bad. And her all-nighters were really all-*weekers*. She had perfect snowlike skin, piercing blue eyes, and less than zero body fat, except for in exactly the right places. I swear some of her mini-skirts were really table napkins posing as skirts. For all appearances' sake, she was flawless.

The weird part, though, is that she treated me like I was a threat to her. I really just wanted to do the job: run her stupid errands, be able to smoke weed all day undetected, and get paid. But instead of acting carefree, cavalier, and cool—I was desperate to please her. I was just so totally afraid of messing up. So afraid, in fact, that I was more likely to go to work puking out of the car window than call in sick. If she wanted a cheaper plane ticket, I told United Airlines my grandpa had just died.

I remember one time, she got on an art kick during one of her coke binges, and she made all these collages. They consisted of pictures of her and her boyfriend and her boyfriend's family (they happen to be Hollywood royalty) on vacation. Instead of gluing the pictures on the paper, she used scotch tape—*over* everybody's face. So, when it came time for me to color copy and blow up her masterpieces, you didn't pay attention to the boyfriend's Academy Award–winning sister, but rather the jagged pieces of tape across her face. She told me to scrape off every bit of the scotch tape without fucking up the pictures. Of course she'd used originals, and of course the only tool that could do the job was an X-Acto knife. I was like a paranoid med student on meth. I tried. I really tried. But I just ended up giving the Academy Award–winning sister her first nose job.

Even though working for her was ulcer-causing because I never knew what to expect and I should have quit, I felt sorry for her. So, I stayed on. Too long. I like to ride things till the wheels come off. She was going through a rough patch. I told myself it wasn't personal. She had recently been fired from a big movie, the high-rolling boyfriend had just dumped her in a gloriously dramatic way, and she couldn't seem to get her shit together enough to make it to auditions. In fact, she'd missed the same important audition three times in a row because of "food poisoning." Whose fault was that? *Mine*. She would hole up for days in the bungalows of the Beverly Hills Hotel despite my best efforts—alarm setting, map drawing, warnings, warnings that warnings were coming. She stood up casting directors multiple times. I suppose our lives were kind of crumbling at the same time. Of course, for her this meant drinking SKYY vodka as opposed to Ketel One, and for me it meant drinking fingernail polish remover instead of boxed wine.

Anyhoo, the breakup meant she'd have to move out of the boyfriend's place, and I was now responsible for emptying out a huge house in Beverly Hills of all her rich-lady regalia. The dishes, the linens, the closet (closets) full of Prada, Versace, Formica, cornkachi whatever-the-fuck, and all 150 million wall sconces. Of course you can't leave the wall sconces! We're in the middle of a Hollywood breakup here, people! He was lucky we didn't drive away and throw a match behind us! Of course, if we'd done that I'd have made my quick getaway in my circa 1973 VW van. I may as well have driven myself to the police station. All the while she would be crossing the Mexican border in her brand-new Land Rover.

Back to packing. I needed to spend the night in order to greet the movers first thing in the morning, and while I finished the packing, she hung out in the upstairs bedroom listening to Fiona Apple's "On the Bound" on a loop. When it came time for me to try to get a few hours' sleep, I lay down on a bare mattress in a guest room. I was fucking beat. I didn't

want to be doing this shit anymore. And goddamnit, I didn't
have a blanket. I reached into one of the boxes and pulled out
. . . yes! Something I could use as a blanket . . . *nope*. It was one
of her fucking napkin skirts. Well . . . my *feet* would be warm.
Okay, my foot would be warm. *Good night*. Tomorrow I would
muster up the courage to quit. *After* she paid me.

It was then that I heard, "Morgan, you can't sleep in
there. Just sleep in here—I have the pillows." I paused at
this because a) yes, she did have the pillows, b) she was my
boss, and c) this was just about the nicest she'd ever been, so I
wanted to make sure it was really her and not an alien inhab-
iting her body. So I went upstairs.

I opened Shana's bedroom door to find her in a tank top
and underwear. She was drinking straight out of a bottle
of Ketel One, and some weed and coke were on the bedside
table while a vibrator was lying oh so inconspicuously beside
her. You heard me: *a vibrator*. Don't all bosses lie around with
vibrators? I pretended not to see it. She offered me the bottle,
and I took a big swig. She offered me the weed, and I took a
huge hit and blew smoke rings to be cool. I don't know. I was
nervous and weirded out. But I didn't know how to leave,
and I didn't know how to stay. So I stayed physically and left
mentally. The story of my life. I proceeded to get *fucked up*.
After a while we were actually laughing together. I was still
pretending the vibrator wasn't there, but it was staring at
me through its eye. Maybe there was no eye, but all I could
think was, Fakepenis fakepenis fakepenis. There was something different about her this night; she was being way more
girly and way less bossy. . . .

And then it happened. She kissed me. My eyes were open, hers were closed, and my eyeballs felt like they were going to burst out of my head. Was this really happening—was she really kissing me? And then I thought, I can do this. This is fine. I had kissed a girl once before, in college, after getting super drunk. It's just kissing.

And then she handed me the vibrator.

She asked me softly in my ear to use it on her, but I had never, you know, checked out another lady's business! I hardly understood my own anatomy! My head was rushing with: She's your boss, she's beautiful, it's a new life experience, will I get a raise? I can't reject her; I might not get paid . . . I'm an hourly employee—is this overtime? And—this may sound crazy, because you know, I *have* a vagina—but I had no idea where to put, set, stick (!?) the vibrator. I was *frozen*. Then Shana took my chin in her hand and raised my ear to her mouth. I thought she was going to give me some instruction or, even better, tell me, "Hey, never mind, don't worry about it. We can just drink the rest of this vodka and watch movies." But no, instead, she said in an uncharacteristically self-conscious voice, "I have a really long labia." And then, as if she hadn't just said the most shocking and unsexy words I had ever heard, she softly but firmly escorted me back down . . . *there*. Now I am fucking terrified. I was at a loss when I thought it was your good ole fashioned regular-length vagina. Can I just say that the word "length" should never be used in terms of female sexual organs? Men, yes; Women, *no*. Where is my trapdoor? Do I fake a seizure? No, I can't. It's too late now. I took another giant swig of Ketel

One and ventured into unchartered personal assistant territory. I did it. Just like everything else she had asked me to do. And she wasn't exaggerating. Even I, who had very little experience with any labia, including my own, knew that this labia was astonishing. But I figured, how bad can it be? Let me just say, it can be very, very bad. I fumbled around. I did what I thought I was supposed to. She seemed pleased. . . . I don't fucking know.

The next morning the movers rang the doorbell, and I helped empty out every room but hers. I let her sleep. When I absolutely had to, I woke her up. I tried to pretend like nothing had happened. (No trace of judgment about the labia either.) I reminded her about her appointments that day and that her bungalow was ready for check-in. Instead of her usual brush-off she said, "Can you come with me? What're you doing today?" Oh my God, I thought. Who's *the boss* now?

I would love to say I quit gracefully, but two days later Shana checked herself into treatment, and I went to work for the ex-boyfriend. Who I later slept with.

CHAPTER 7

WORDS OF MOUTH

when you have to swallow more than your pride

History's finest orators have ignited the passions of entire generations with the manifestations of their mouths, while those less orally adept are better remembered for clumsy slips of the tongue. Often seen as sex's most selfless act, oral challenges the idiom "'tis better to give than to receive." Unless you're a member of the Cliterati* or the Phallisophers,* partaking of the forbidden fruit of the loom can have consequences. The authors featured here recount some oral encounters that really sucked.

FACE-FUCKED BY AN ELEPHANT MAN

by Security Guard, Female

The year was 2007; the place, New York City. It was the first year of what I like to call "graduate school," which was really just a job I held as a security guard at a lamp store. The sun had set, and just as I was about to hang up my lobby hero hat for the day, a faint whisper echoed from the empty showroom behind me.

"Namaste," a man's voice said.

He was an older gentleman. Caucasian. He wore tight black jeans and a billowy white blouse. He sported a low ponytail. He introduced himself as an artist, a sculptor of nature, "man versus wild." He then presented me with a post-card, a sample of his work, and there oddly pictured, in various media of clay, cotton, and paper clips were sculptures of elephants. Scribbled underneath: "The Elephant Man." We said our good-byes. I had been only mildly impressed, but after an online search I discovered the Elephant Man was Internet famous!

Forty-five minutes later I was knocking at his door.

Elephant Man answered the door barefoot, wearing something flowy and made of gauze. Some type of classical Southeast Asian tribal beat bongoed on the speakers in the background. He insisted I make myself comfortable on the Indian rickshaw he was using for a couch while he poured me an expensive glass of pinot he had brought back from the Australian outback. While I drank that, Elephant Man sipped a steaming cup of kava kava tea out of a giant gourd. We engaged in some chitchat and soon I was drunk. Him? Sober.

I agreed to take a tour of his apartment, which, of course, ended in his bedroom with me half-naked, giggling in his bed.

One thing led to another, and soon we had neatly rounded the bases, but just when we were about to head toward home, my insides quivered with hesitation.

Perhaps it was seeing his old elephant ears close up, cracked and flappy like two raw pieces of breakfast ham.

Maybe it was because of the musty smell of his body odor mixed with some type of organic cologne, which together smelled of patchouli oil and aged Gouda.

Or, perchance it was because right then he flashed me a toothy smile with a near-rotten snaggletooth—similar to a tusk—I hadn't noticed before. Suddenly, all I could see through the darkness were black and white images of David Lynch's 1980s classic, with my conscience screaming, Don't have sex with the Elephant Man! Don't have sex with the Elephant Man!

I awkwardly used his balls to steer his penis away from my vagina and began a comfortable pickle between third and second; however, I could sense his frustration, because like a frisky jungle mating ritual, our parts began to aggressively tangle with one another. First, he reared me from the front, which I countered by using my arms in a four-count slide to the back. Second, he mounted me from behind, which I deflected by using my ass as a catapult, springing him into the air. And from the side he tried to distract me by sticking his finger up my butthole, but he was no match for my squeeze-pump-thrust, which landed me once again on my back and him determining his next move.

And then began a little foul play. Before I knew it, Elephant Man was slowly sliding his penis/trunk up my stomach, then my chest, until it landed gently on my cheek. Surely this was a mistake! I tried another shake-off, but like a lazy jungle snake it stayed right where it wanted.

Then he started to fuck my face.

This was not like anything I had experienced before. I'd been downtown many times; I frankly consider myself a bit of an expert in the area, but this time I was not downtown; he was uptown, and I was midtown. I tried to steer him away by grabbing hold of his sagging ass, but my fingers became lost in the soft folds of his wrinkled skin. For a moment I was taken with the little fella, until a mound of his gray pubis jammed up my nose and almost suffocated me to death. Soon I realized that the more I tried to squeeze, slap, and tug, the more it must have seemed like I was game.

So, like a force-fed anorexic, I took it. One. Piece. At a time. As his old, old, old elephant balls continued to slap me in the chin, I was reminded of Charlie, my childhood shih tzu, the only other time my face had wrestled with this amount of moist hair and flesh. And thanks to little Charlie's image I was able to hold out until Elephant Man was finished. But you know what they say: It's hard to ignore the elephant in the room when you're choking on its cock.

How was this going to end? I had heard stories: pearl necklace, cum mask, cum fart cocktail. But, when I was pretty sure this was only going to end one way, I swallowed hard and gave it the old college try. Never underestimate your ability to beer-bong, because one day it might save your life . . . like it did mine.

CUDDLEWHORE

by Beth Littleford

The first time I engaged in prostitution, I was sixteen.

His name was Ian McCabe, and he was my age. Also, he was kind of chubby and kind of smelly. But not as in "that poor chubby, smelly kid"—no, he was way cooler than that. The "chubby" was like his whole body—lips, belly, butt—was a little bit bee-stung. Which was feasibly sort of sexy. And the "smelly" was that hippie BO, which was feasibly sort of cool. Basically, he was a rebel: He didn't believe in capitalism, he didn't believe in religion, he didn't believe in soap.

He had heavy-lidded eyes and a mellow grin. He always seemed rumpled and sleepy like he'd just awoken from a pleasant nap. In reality, he was just stoned and in clothes he'd pulled out of the dirties. But I was seeing him through rose-colored glasses, because Ian had the feature I found most attractive in a man: He didn't want me. In fact, he wanted my best friend, Laurel. He'd told me this after we fooled around for the first time, and I'd taken it in stride, even passing the information on to her and offering him up. She'd squinched up her nose at the thought. I know she didn't want to insult my taste outright—she was always my steadfast supporter—but . . . eww. Laurel was president of our class and a cheerleader. Bottom line, Laurel believed in capitalism, religion, and soap.

I'd started that school year shooting for student council and homecoming, arriving to school every day in full makeup, matching shoes and purse, and a complete ensemble of rings, necklace, earrings, *and* bracelet (gold or silver, never a mix). But it quickly became more than I could manage. I began wearing only men's clothes. Huaraches I picked up on the beach. A tattered pair of jeans from a guy friend. No bra. Boxer shorts and pajama bottoms rolled over twice at the waist. Almost all were clothes that had belonged to my dad, clothes he wasn't around anymore to wear.

You see, that first week of school my junior year, my dad had taken my little brother on a fishing trip into the Alaskan wilderness for his twelfth birthday. Their tiny pontoon plane sank into the Alaskan bay, and they were never seen again.

I wouldn't talk to anyone about it. I didn't mention either of them, but I wore my dad; I took his T-shirts like "World's Greatest Dad" and "Forty and Fabulous," slashed off the arms and flashdanced the neck, and made them my wardrobe.

And I started smoking heavily and publicly—Salem Lights, whose menthol crystals were said to cut up your lungs like fiberglass.

So I found myself gravitating toward Ian's group. The grunge group, before grunge existed.

One day, a bunch of us drove out to spend the night at our friend's beach house in New Smyrna Beach, Florida. Beach houses in New Smyrna were basically double-wides on stilts, three dirt roads over from the ocean. We arrived late, had a round of tequila shots, and then retired. Ian took the master bedroom. I'm not sure why he thought himself entitled to it, but no one questioned it. Laurel and I took the twin beds across the hall.

As soon as the lights were out, I knew I'd go across the hall to his room. I guess I thought I'd try again to find myself some lovin'. Never mind that he'd made it clear he had no lovin' for me. Life for me then was all about the denial. It had only been a month since I'd lost half my family, and I wasn't about to face that. So I snuck into Ian's room.

I stood against the door and said I was lonely. But I didn't want to fool around; I only wanted to be held. He invited me in and we lay on the bed and talked. He said his father was away, leading a trip to Mount Kilimanjaro and making everyone read the Hemingway short story of the same name, and had I read Hemingway?

"Oh, sure, well, like what? *The Old Man and the Sea.* Yeah, yeah, I mean that's Hemingway, right?"

He loved Somerset Maugham, he said. Did I know *The Razor's Edge*?

"What, like, with Bill Murray? Right, yeah, no, based on the book, I know, yeah, right. . . . Sort of existential angst and opium dens, right?"

He brought up Laurel, declaring that he was in love with her. "If you pierced her," he said, "a beam of golden light would shoot out."

"Yeah, yeah," I shrugged.

I had to admit, it was true. Laurel *was* golden, beautiful, emotionally intact.

Laurel would never do what I did next.

Which was sell myself to Ian. Technically, it wasn't sex for money; it was more of a barter. I said I just needed to be held tenderly till I fell asleep. He said he just needed a blowjob. So we struck a bargain, a straight-up deal: a hum-mer* for hugs.

He pulled his Guatemalan serape hoodie over his head and pulled down his jeans. A puff of ashy dust billowed up as they hit the floor by the bed in a heap, and I remembered that Ian would tap his cigarette ash onto his jeans, rub it in, and explain that ash is "a natural deodorizer." He was left laying there, all baby fat in tightie whities, except these particular ones were old enough to be called "loosey whities," and dis-colored enough to be called "loosey grayies." And with a faint beige tint in the crotch-al region.

He pulled them down and his penis boinged up, perpen-dicular to his body. I slid myself lower down his torso and was hit with his musk. Not the intoxicating musk you read about in a romance novel, more the suffocating musk you encounter at a petting zoo. I adjusted.

I'd never seen a penis face-to-face before, so I thought I'd get to know it a little first.

"Hello. I like your hat. Is that a jaunty beret? Or are you a fireman? . . . Oh!" I said as I squeezed. "Spongy! What? I was just warming up to it. . . . Okay, I'll start."

I took a tentative lick, as if testing an ice cream flavor I wasn't so sure about.

Then another. And another.

"Three licks. It takes three licks to get to the center of a t—"

No response.

"You don't remember the tootsie pop commercial with the owl? 'How many licks? Three licks.' He had the English accent. . . . "

Apparently, he'd never seen the commercial. Or wasn't in the mood for TV nostalgia.

"Okay, you know, I'm new to this, so what do I do, just cover my teeth with my . . . ? And just, what, descend?"

So I descended. His hand stroked my hair. "Oh, that's sweet," I thought. "I must be doing okay if he's petting the back of my head." But what I thought was a pet was really a push that jammed his jaunty beret right up into my esophagus. He proceeded to bounce my head like it was a basketball and he was a Harlem Globetrotter.

"Breathe through your nose, breathe through your nose," I kept telling myself. The only problem with that was the odor. Yep, apparently balls have sweat glands. But I squelched my gag reflex and performed adequately enough, because the next thing I knew . . . "Ack!" I gagged, and gulped, relieved that it was finally over.

Which it wasn't.

"Oh my God, there's more than one . . . spurt?" I tried to gulp some more. "Bathroom?" I asked, mouth still somewhat full. "Be right back."

When I returned, he was lying back with his hands behind his head and his eyes closed. I snuggled up alongside him and laid my head on his chest, nuzzling up into his armpit. Then I nuzzled more aggressively, enough to try to force his arm around me. I made several attempts at this. And . . . nothing.

He brought my hand up to his ear and whispered something. "Oh, what's that? Your mom used to rub your earlobes? Oh, to help you fall asleep? Oh, that's sweet. Sure, I can. Like that . . . ?" I began to rub his lobes between my thumb and forefinger, in a slow, circular motion.

"You know, I love that we're sharing this intimate thing, the earlobe thing, but—I have to say—this doesn't really count as you holding me while I fall asleep. You'd actually have to be holding me in some way for that to, you know, count. . . . Ian? . . .

Ian?"

That's when I heard the snore.

And that's when I got furious. Not with Ian. With myself.

"Stupid, stupid, stupid," I hissed.

It would be years before I'd have any compassion for my younger self, my inner cuddlewhore. A compassion I would also feel acutely for the girls called sluts—the Monica Lewinskys. Because I *get* Monica Lewinsky. I get the desperate acts of a broken girl.

I would do this kind of thing again and again . . . and again over the next decade. The only difference would be that I'd now learned the most important lesson of prostitution: always get paid up front.

PS: In case you were wondering, a broken girl can heal. I'm now a longtime happily married lady with a kid. But, truth be told, I still use sex as a bartering tool. *First* we see the chick flick. *Then* he gets the blowjob. And everyone goes to bed happy.

CAN'T BLOW ME LOVE

by Laura Kindred

> "Look—it's a nerd herd!"
> — *Can't Buy Me Love*

I went to high school in the nineties. But I grew up in the eighties—the decade of some of the finest and tackiest cinematic meditations on the high school predicament. The same old tired plotlines recycled for their archetypal appeal: the graduation party; the last summer before college; the boy in love with a girl out of his league who's been dating the same douchebag* for years—but wait! He just dumped her so he can be free to chase tail all summer long; the nerd with the elaborate scientific plot to get back at the jock who gave him swirlies every day after gym class. . . .

In my school of fish, we were *all* nerds. I attended an institution for overachievers—the kind of place that refers to itself as an "academy" in lieu of a "high school." We were *all* kids who, if we were anywhere else, would be getting swirlies and wedgies; we wouldn't be getting "some." Instead of whip-its and hand jobs behind the backstop on Saturdays, we would crush up and snort Priya's Ritalin prescription, then cab it to Denny's and discuss Proust.

As such, we had to make do with a somewhat underdeveloped level of sexy. The hormones were there, but standards had to be adjusted. Our love was not a cinematic love. Our coming of age was more of a stumble. An outsider might ask,

What about that four-eyed girl with the unibrow who does Civil War reenactments? Does she really give heart palpitations to the runty boy in the Boba Fett T-shirt with the first, soft sprouts of a mustache feathering under his nose?

The answer is yes. You can't fish marlin in a freshwater lake, so trout starts to taste pretty good.

In any society, there are always a few who float to the top. One of our floaters was a guy who went by the dubious name of "Ripper." I think his actual name was something like William Aldridge Plymouth III, but he went by Ripper. Ripper had long brown hair that was cut razor straight across the bottom and perfectly round nostrils that faced more out than down. He was kind of sporty—I don't even think he had an inhaler—and gave and received a lot of high fives that actually hit their targets. He'd have been shark chum in any other environment . . . but at Exeter he was Emilio Estevez. He dated a girl who had the nerve to be bitchy in spite of being a nerd, and was therefore perceived as cool. She was a stoner, and also in student government. She was rumored to have slept with one of the philosophy faculty. There was no competing with Lila Clearfield.

In any society, there are also those who feed at the bottom. Dweebs among dweebs. I had happily settled into this sediment, because I enjoyed welding and cutting my own hair into a jagged bowl and was grotesquely skinny and passionate about Camus. I ate oranges and Cheerios alone under a tree on the quad because I was too agoraphobic to eat in the dining hall.

There was no Ripper to my Lila. There wasn't even a

Poindexter to my Agnes. I compulsively drew eyeballs all over my jeans—a habit I would later find out to be a symptom of schizophrenia—but I drew no stares from the opposite sex. My first and last attempt to initiate a romantic encounter in high school came and went when, at the urging of my best friend, I called a boy named Riley and asked him if he wanted to "hang out sometime." He sounded so mortified, I just hung up.

So you can imagine my surprise when, at an end-of-year party at the sprawling Vermont estate of an inordinately wealthy classmate, I found myself being chatted up by Ripper. Lila had dumped him a few weeks earlier, so naturally he was scoping out his evening conquest, but to revisit a metaphor, he was swimming in trout, and I was tripe. Sure, I'd made a few improvements and gained a couple of inches, but I was all raw material. Again, this is a high school movie plot mainstay: Cindy's friends are baffled by her choice of Ronnie and they're right to be; there are other factors at play.

So I was understandably suspicious when Ripper made a point of talking to me . . . brushing hair out of my face . . . gently placing a hand on my back. He walked away momentarily to get me a Solo Cup of beer from the keg, and my friend, the one from earlier, pleaded with me not to do anything untoward, declaring Ripper a "walking clap dispenser."

But she'd long since discredited herself as romantic advisor with the Riley incident. Maybe Ripper was on something, maybe he was all tore up about Lila, but I was going to carpe his diem. Because who knew when, or if, this chance would come again. I was willing to be the baffling half of the mismatched couple—the sad "why *her*?"—for an evening. And I allowed Ripper to lead me by the hand into the middle of a large field, away from the surprised eyeballs of my classmates. Oh, prophetic denim.

In hindsight I think the experience Ripper and I had in that field was a little bit like a child molestation . . . for both of us. In part because he touched me and made me touch him in places and ways I'd rather not have, and in part because I had the skill and experience of a small child. He would distract me with the stars—"Look! It's Orion!" (he was in astronomy club)—and slip a hand in my shirt while I was trying to take in the celestial wonder. He'd place my hand on his bulging jeans, and I'd look at him blankly until he gave up and undid his own fly. I announced to him petulantly when he went for mine that my pants were staying on.

"But I'll give you a blowjob, okay?"

This must have been quite a moment for Ripper. On the one hand, he was being told point-blank he was going to get his dick sucked. On the other, it was being offered deadpan by a girl who was clearly volunteering to fellate him only in order to avoid actual sex. Not exactly an ego boost. And he must have felt like he was doing me a favor, which would have made my desperate compromise doubly unanticipated. He made one attempt to make it right before accepting.

"We don't have to have sex. But I can touch you."

I wrinkled up my nose and he relented. We removed his pants and I proceeded to "blow" him.

You know how sometimes, if you're drinking a milk shake or a soda, in order to look sensual or just for fun, instead of taking the straw with your fingers and placing it between your lips, you'll actually attempt to curl your tongue around the side of the straw and loop it into your mouth, hands-free? At this point in my life I'd had a lot of sodas, a good number of milk shakes, and zero penises in my mouth, so this is how I tried to administer oral sex to Ripper. His penis lay prone against his stomach, and I went in from the side and tried to slide my tongue underneath it and lift it into an upright position that I might then be able to place my mouth around. When this didn't prove very fruitful, I tried the other side, and then attempted to go in from the top and sort of vacuum it up, but this required me to jam my forehead and nose into Ripper's stomach. I tried the right side again, and after a lot of trial and error, Ripper reached down with his own hand (mine were by my sides) and held his penis up in a position I could get my mouth around.

Thanks, Ripper!

Rather than take over manually, I continued to try to keep him in place with just my mouth. Not that I was in a place to question his aptitude, but I will mention that Ripper, while considerably more experienced than I, was inexperienced enough to hump my gullet until I gagged and had to retreat, so that we had to repeatedly start from zero. I, who had managed model studentry in some of the most gratuitously difficult curricula available to teenage-kind, was too dim to pick up on one visual cue: Use your hands.

Finally Ripper just wrapped his own hands around it and let me go to town on the top. This is how we managed to bring him to climax. It was so clumsy it must have required extensive creative mental imagery on his part, which also must have been why he was too distracted to warn me when the surge was working. Our encounter ended with a sputter, a gurgling choking noise, and a moment of silence.

"Thank you," he said as he stroked my hair. Then he waited for me to thank him. I didn't.

That was eleven years ago. My life resembles a popular movie plotline in one additional way. Recently I attended my ten-year high school reunion. Ten years can do a lot to a person, and while I am no cover girl, managing to be one of the few of my classmates not to have become fat and/or bald was grounds for alumni celebrity. I was, dare I say it, a catch. I saw Ripper at the reunion, ruddy and Buddha-bellied from beer and a life of inherited excess. When he staggered up to me at the cocktail reception and asked in a suggestive way if I remembered the last time we'd seen each other, I laughed and affirmed I did, indeed, remember the no-hands blowjob. Life treats me well enough these days. I have learned how to use my hands. I have learned how to use my mouth. And with the latter, I am ordering the marlin.

"Nerds, jocks. My side, your side. It's all bullshit.
It's hard enough just trying to be yourself."
— *Can't Buy Me Love*

CHAPTER 8

GOING AGAINST THE GAY

not what nature intended

The question of whether homosexuality is a lifestyle choice you nurture or an inherent aspect of your nature has been debated by the greatest psychologists, genealogists, and gynecologists of our time. We hope to shed some light on this subject by revealing intimate portrayals of what happens when one decides to ignore the innate sexual voice within or forcefully tries to change another's. This chapter proves that not only is sexual preference an ingrained element of one's being, it is not to be fucked with . . . faggot.

COMING IN

by Wally Marzano-Lesnevich

"You want to jump my bones, don't you?" she asked provocatively from across the couch. I looked at her: womanly curves, large lips, flowing dark brown hair. A good figure, with flesh in all the right places. Yes, I wanted to jump her bones.

There was only one teeny, *tiny* little problem.

I was gay.

Oops.

How one navigates from being an ass ninja* to this particular moment of desperately wanting to bone a chick is not a graceful story, as the first part of this sentence illustrates. Looking back through the spectacular string of bad decisions that constitute the B-movie that is my life, I find the decision to come out of the closet to be the most impressively, awesomely, spectacularly bad of all. It comes with its own built-in life lessons, in sizes small (you should never come out of the closet to everyone you know after you've only kissed one boy), medium (a childhood pre-cougar obsession with Jennifer Aniston can never really be replaced), and large (men do not have breasts).

I was twenty-three when I made this decision and a senior in college—theatre school, appropriately—and some might say old enough to know better. In the rearview mirror of my pubescence one would see: a botched attempt at sex with a slightly older woman whose crude campus nickname was "Smelly Hairs," one particularly emotionally scarring life

experience that would sink this piece faster than a nude picture of "Smelly Hairs," a semester in London, wonderfully tolerant friends, and heaping amounts of ecstasy.

I know what you're thinking: That would make me gay
too. Oh, wait, no, you're not thinking that? Hmm.

I'm, alas, not facile enough a writer to explain, in mere
words, how reading the *New York Times*, drinking fine wines,
and having a healthy knowledge of the Great American
Songbook before one leaves college can lead one to believe he
is gay. (I suppose we could add using the word "alas" without
irony to that list.) I do know it would've been a hell of a lot easier to just come to the conclusion that I was old before my time.

So there I was, in merry old England with a gay flat-
mate (aren't they all?), trying to figure out why I wasn't good
enough at Marlowe and Shakespeare. I battled nightly with
my demons, drank all I could get my hands on (I did mention
it was England, right?), and ultimately came to the conclusion that I was gay.

Again, major oops.

Oddly enough, what immediately followed was the least
painful part of this strange eight-year odyssey: the coming out. Really, if you've been raised in a liberal, staunchly
Democratic family and performed in theatre your whole life,
coming out is a joy. You get heaped with praise for not really
doing anything, you validate your interests and everyone's
beliefs, and you go to sleep at night not feeling guilty for
watching reruns of *Dawson's Creek,* because, hey—you're gay.

No, what was painful, literally and figuratively, was the
sex.

Ladies and gentlemen, I have been your intrepid reporter in the field, and let me tell you, sex with a man and sex with a woman is completely, irrevocably different. My inability to ejaculate with a man probably should've been my first clue that I was not actually gay.

I returned from London and promptly started dating the one boy I had kissed. He was, I later saw, the most delicate and feminine creature a gay man could date. After a few futile nights spent rubbing our bodies together with very little to show for it, I panicked and took him to lunch and ended our erstwhile relationship. (Just for the record, while I'm rather fucked up, my self-loathing does not extend to others; I paid for both of our grilled cheese sandwiches. Gayest. Meal. Ever.)

What followed were truly the worst sexual experiences a closeted straight man could ever have: drunkenly kissing a go-go boy; e-mailing with a guy from Craigslist only to realize he's your neighbor; making out with a fetching blond girl and a bisexual dude on a dance floor, and trying to figure out how we could get rid of the bisexual dude.

I briefly dated a very nice Latin boy who was a musical theatre dancer. A very nice blond boy I met volunteering at a film festival. A very nice boy who was a schoolteacher and lived right up the street. All of these very nice boys shared two traits: I simply could not ejaculate in front of them, and none of them had boobs.

But I did get to continually come out to people and confound people's expectations. I loved baseball! I didn't know how to dress! I sounded so masculine! (I know, I know:

exclamation marks don't back that last part up.) And really, if you've only lived in blue states, people—at weddings, in bars—are simply delighted to meet a nice gay guy.

In fact, I blame the tolerant blue-staters. Damn 'em.

After a few years of getting wasted, not having sex, and tossing one off to forty-five-second clips of blond-haired, big-breasted women on the Internet (I'm telling you, you have to be really committed to ignore clues like this), I found myself with a rather large problem: I had been gay for several years, my family and friends knew and were fabulous with it, and I was spending all my time fantasizing about women. I started sneaking off to bars, drinking delicious liquid courage, and smooching with girls. Girls?! What the hell was wrong with me?

I would say it didn't matter. I would say it meant nothing. I would explain to myself that I was indeed gay. I owned sweater vests. I read Michael Cunningham. Hell, I can quote *Sleepless in Seattle*.

But deep down I knew I had a problem: I was straight.

I had failed again. I had failed at cock sucking, butt pirating, at being the gay man to my best friend's fag hag. (I had once drunkenly kissed her. Oops.) I had failed at being gay.

This stark failure came into relief at a friend's wedding last October. While it wasn't a gay wedding, it was a very gay wedding—lots of single gay guy friends of the bride, and as the token gay guy friend of the groom I was being set up with one of them. Excellent. A nice guy, some good old-fashioned gay sex (even if I didn't quite grasp what that was), and then we'd spend our nights together reading Noël Coward aloud and drinking Chablis.

Only there I was, standing near the appetizers and minding my own damn gay business (I was wearing suspenders, for goodness sake!) when a striking blonde with short hair and a glimmer in her eyes walked up to me. Oh, boy.

"You're very attractive," she said to me. Huh? What? "You're very direct," I shot back. As if to confirm my line of dialogue, her next one was, "Are you gay or straight?"

I hemmed and hawed; I did the gay-but-questioning, thinking-of-having-sex-with-a-woman thing. (That's a thing, right?) She lost interest, she moved on; the better question was, Why hadn't I?

She got very drunk and made out with a groomsman who had been pining after someone else. I found her later and, befitting our new relationship where we speak just subtext, asked her why she had hooked up with that guy if she found me attractive.

Now it was her turn to be surprised. "You said you were gay." I said we could still kiss, so we did, and as we did I thought to myself, Why the hell am I running from this thing I want so much?! I thought we were going to get out of there and have glorious drunk-wedding heterosexual sex.

Instead, she threw up. A friend sent her home in a cab. Great. I had kissed a cute girl and she ralphed. Now I was definitely gay. Only I was the kind of gay guy who desperately wanted to sleep with women, which made me, well . . . no kind of gay guy at all. Shoot.

And so now, eight years of trying to be gay later, I found myself across from this beautiful woman who knew my story and who was still, somehow, willing to sleep with me.

To this day I have no idea what went through my mind as we slept together. No doubt it was the worst, missionary, virgin, disappointing, I'd-rather-have-a-glass-of-pinot-grigio-and-watch-*True Blood* sex she ever had, but at that moment I was a champion. I was Albert Pujols! I was Ernest Hemingway! I was—

Done. I was done. I came. As we engaged in awkward post-coitus banter, she asked me what my favorite part of the female anatomy was, and I stupidly, collegially, answered, "Boobs." Had I the moment to do again, I would speak the truth: "All of it."

I knew that my career as a gay man had ended, and I was about to embark on a much more exciting and more expensive chapter in my life that would be accompanied by its own thrilling wonder and utter madness. I was going to date women.

Addendum: I have, ahem, been making up for lost time. To quote a friend: "I've never seen anyone go from gay to douche in such a short period of time."

GET YOUR TITTY OFF MY THIGH

by Tymberlee Hill

There is a blissful and beautiful gated community in upstate New York called Chautauqua. It was in a summer stock theatre company there that I met Elise Cassar. Elise was extraordinary. She was the star of the summer and *everyone* loved her. *I* loved her. But the most magnetic quality about Elise was her unrivaled sexuality. The human incarnation of copulation, this woman reeked of sex.

Now, to be quite honest, I had no idea what I would do with her once I had her, but that didn't stop me from wanting her more than anything. So I, like everyone else, spent the summer trying to get close to Elise. And all to no avail. Exhausted, dejected, and cloaked in failure, I was ready to throw in the proverbial towel when fate stepped in—we became scene partners.

Blessed with this rare opportunity, I used every minute of that time to make her love me. This included the usual shenanigans: coincidentally sitting next to her at *every* meal; offering up astonishing insights into the brilliance of her work during scene study class; walking nonchalantly next to her and sayin' things that are certain to bring two people together, "Oh my God, I totally have that same shirt at home!" (I didn't); professing a love for music that she loved (I didn't); and laughing heartily—yes, faith—heartily at every syllable that fell from her mouth.

It's important to note that, unlike Elise, I had never gone

all the way with another girl. I mean, I had noticed women before. Of course. But I recognize that, as lovely as they are, I am still strickly dickly.* There's really no getting around it. Cunnilingus? Yes. Finger fun? Sure. But after that, if you don't try to knock the back outta me . . . we've wasted our time. See, I consider myself a lesbian from the waist *up.* Meaning: I've kissed my fair share of girls, squeezed my fair share of titties . . . and I like it.

Moving on.

We're creeping up on the end of the summer, and Elise says to me, "Can you believe we only have four more days?" Summer stock translation: we need to hurry up and fuck. So later on that night, we're having our obligatory seventies-themed party in the paint shop. We're all outside smokin', drinkin', and dancin' around barefoot in circles and shit, when suddenly Elise reaches out to me, grabs me by the collar of my shirt, pulls me to her, and says, "Kiss me." And I did.

And the night continues. And the drinkin' continues. And the drugs continue. And as the evening begins to drag deliriously into morning, Elise reaches out a second time, pulling me into the bathroom and locking the door behind us. Now she is all over me. We're on the floor, against the wall, on top of the sink. She takes two steps away from me. She meets my eyes seductively and says, quite frankly, "I wanna fuck you. Meet me back in the dorm in fifteen minutes."

So, fifteen minutes pass, and I find myself walkin' up the gilded stairwell into a warm room of candlelight and sandalwood. I let myself in and make my way over to the bed. Elise comes out of the bathroom. I rise to meet her. She takes my

face in her hands and begins to kiss me with such passion
and urgency that I believe for a few minutes that I might
actually be in love with her.

Our clothes start flying. We fall back on the bed, and then,
just then, I receive the most ridiculous finger fuck *of my life*.
She cradles me like a bowling ball, her two middle fingers
moving inside me, while she simultaneously runs her thumb
across my clit faster than any electronic device I have ever
owned. And just when I think I'm about to come, I stop—
because Elise Cassar tells me she isn't "ready for me to come
yet."

And then, I feel it. It is the tip of her nose and then the
top of her lip dragging slowly down the center of my body. As
she begins to go down, down, down on me, I suddenly think
to myself, Oh my God, I'm about to get head from a lesbian!

And then I think, Oh my God . . . I'm about to get head
from a lesbian?

See, it is in this moment that I realize that I am not ready
for below-the-waist love. But it is too late, because just then—
donk—I feel her titty mush up against the inside of my thigh.
And without thinking, I yell, "Oh my God! Get your titty off
my thigh!" Elise looks up at me in confusion. "What?!"

I said, "Get. Your. Titty. Off. My thigh!"

I sit up abruptly, driving my knee into Elise's chin and
smashing her bottom lip into her top row of teeth. And she is
bleeding now. Like a hemophiliac. I thought she was going to
die. She starts shaking like a drunk in detox and screaming,
"Fuuuuck! Fuuuuuck!"

I turn around to grab some napkins off the desk; instead, I

swat a candle off of it and onto the bed, and now the bed is on fire. I lean over, trying to suffocate the flames with the blanket. But unfortunately, when I leaned in, my weave leaned in too, and now my hair is on fire. I stand there screaming, trying to smack out the flames with my bare hands. Meanwhile Elise is lookin' at me—the way one might look at a person who disfigured her and set her room on fire—and is screaming, "Get out! Get the fuck out!"

So I scooped up my little puddle of clothes and ran out into the hallway. I got dressed and wandered aimlessly back to my dorm. The next day, and for the last few days of stock, Elise ignored me, and quite effectively; she was flawless in her execution. She explained to everyone that her swollen lip was the result of a slip and fall in the shower.

At this point you may be asking yourself, How is this the worst sex of your life? I mean, *you* didn't give someone the bomb fingerblast* and then get kicked in the face. And you would be right. But here's the thing: For all the crap sex I've had, that marked the first and the last time that *I* was the asshole.

HOMOSEXUAL SCHMOMOSEXUAL

by Alison Brie

I went to art school. Now art school is not like regular college. Tai chi was a required course, we had a circus class taught by a bearded lady, and clothing was optional everywhere but the cafeteria. Similarly, the students there are of a different grain. They're very deep and introspective, really open to experimentation of any kind, and they have weird haircuts. In my case, the first year there was fraught with exploration. I learned a lot about the inner workings of me. I learned how to become "a clean sheet of paper"; I learned how to breathe through my coccyx; I learned that pretty much anyone would have sex with me. This at first I thought was because I was "so talented" or "so creative." Later, of course, I realized I was just easy. So I capitalized on it.

Exploring my newfound sexuality, there was, of course, the girl-on-girl action, the crazy threesome with the afros and whips, and the surreal 'shrooms experience where I thought the tree was fondling me but it turned out to be my creepy male roommate with calluses on his hands. . . . Gross. You get the picture. I developed this (possibly misplaced) sexual pride, based solely on the quantity of penetrations of my vagina . . . and not necessarily the quality of the acts therein.

So one afternoon I'm sitting out on the grass with my overly contemplative, self-hating, gay friend Jon, who's recently come out of the closet and thinks it's the worst thing in the world. He hates being gay. He hates that he has to put it in his butt.

He hates the creepy art major with the blond comb-over who wants to lay "his poopy wiener" in his mouth. He just hates everything about it. And I feel really bad for my friend. I want to help him. This was, of course, not the first time I'd had to listen to him complain about the hopelessness of his situation, despite the seemingly endless list of available male suitors I'd brought to his attention. I decide it's time to get to the root of the problem and see exactly what Jon isn't enjoying about his newfound same-sex sex. So I ask him, "Well, Jonathan, how many guys have you had sex with?"

And he's, like, "None, ewww."

I am a bit surprised by that reaction. So I probe deeper. "Oh. Well, how many girls have you had sex with with?"

And he's like, "None, hello?! Ewww."

And I think to myself, well, okay, the solution is blatantly clear. Jonathan needs to have sex! With *me*! Obviously in order to accurately evaluate his sexual preference and come to an informed conclusion, he must explore all viable options. And what if he were to discover he was actually straight? I would have saved him from a life of dysfunctional penetration. Literally my vagina would have been his road to salvation! One can only listen to the despondent rants of a depressed, confused, and sexually ambiguous virgin for so long before one must take action. Plus, who better to show him the ropes than his very own, self-proclaimed captain of coitus, the queen of copulation herself, and not to mention one of his best friends in the whole world?

So I pitch Jon the idea, and though he's a bit reluctant at first, I really give him the hard sell, and next thing you know

we're both frolicking down to my room to grab the last condom from my sock drawer and then hurry down to his room
before the impulse can pass us by.

We get to his room, a plain, ground-floor dorm room—bed,
desk, wide-open space and this big picture window that looks
out at the school pool with those slat blinds that are always
incomplete, always missing those essential two slats, as his
appropriately are. So I close what's left of the blinds and hop
under the covers, he throws on some music and hops in with
me, both of us pumping with adrenaline at our own spon-
taneity, and we're off! We start making out and . . . we continue making out . . . and I tear off my shirt, and I tear off
his shirt, and I rip off my shorts, and I pull off his jeans . . .
and I'm starting to notice a pattern forming in regards to
one person's possible involvement more than the other's. But
I choose to ignore it until . . . I go to put my hands down his
undies and he lets out a shriek so loud and so feminine, it's
like nothing I've heard in the bedroom before. I pull back, a
bit shocked, and ask, "What?"

He's like, "What're you doing?!"

I smile, "I'm going to touch your penis. . . ."

He's like, "*No*, no no no no no no—I can't, um. . . . That's
not . . ."

I'm like, ". . . oh. Um, do we need to have a talk first about
the fundamentals of copulation . . . or?"

He's like, "No, no, I can do this, let's just have a no-hands-
below-the-waist rule. For now."

So, I'm like, "Okay . . . okay, you know what, it's weird,
yes, but I'm the pro here. I want you to be comfortable, so

whatever I can do, it's okay. You're in good hands. I know what I'm doing, and I can . . . not do that for you."

So we start making out again, and slowly but surely, we get back into it; him awkwardly avoiding my breasts; me sensually stroking his . . . arms. And, you know, we go on this way for quite some time with no results down below, until finally I'm like, "Is there anything I can do? I mean, are you sure you don't want to just let me put my mouth on it? Or . . ." And he's like, "No, no, I just think I'm not so comfortable, you know, I feel like people outside can see me, I'm just kind of having trouble getting into it."

Now at this point I probably could have read the subtext here, like, I'm not into this. I'm not really attracted to you at all. 'Cuz I'm gay. But no, I chose to take this as a plea for further instruction. I mean, I'd tackled problems in the bedroom far more challenging than this and always concluded with a happy ending, so to speak.

So I'm like, "Okay, let's brainstorm. Maybe if we put the mattress in the closet, we'll have plenty of privacy." (I failed to see the irony at the time.) But he's okay with it, and so the next thing I know, we're squeezing the mattress onto the floor of this small, dark closet and we get in there and he's like, "One more thing. I think also you should get stoned. I just think I'll feel more comfortable if you're kind of out of it, ya know, so I can like, do my own thing. . . ."

Now this gave me pause. I was suddenly a little worried. I mean, what were the real motives here? Was he going to wait till I was "out of it" and try to wiggle it into my butt? Did he want to dress me like a boy and sodomize me in secret?

I momentarily pondered my predicament. Was I losing my erotic edge? Had I finally found an envelope I could not push? No! We had gone too far for me to back down now, and I wasn't about to let this little fairy destroy my hard-earned sexual legacy; I've made out with Mormon chicks, for Christ's sake! Luckily, I had my affinity for pot on my side, and the idea of free drugs outweighed any long-term insecurity.

So I say, "Sure! Sounds great! Anything you want."

He's like, "Great! I'll go find better music to set the mood!"

So I'm smoking, I get good and high, and he comes back very excited, like, "Oh my God, I found the perfect song: Madonna's 'Erotica.'" Now . . . this may have been another moment that should have inspired hesitation, but actually I was really excited about it, 'cuz I was stoned, and he was really excited about it. 'Cuz he's gay. So he gets in the closet with me—literally and figuratively—and we're both into it now, like movin' and touchin' our . . . selves. And before we know it, he has liftoff! So he gets the condom on and I get on him and we're *doing it! We're actually doing it!* And we're into it. That's right. We grind and bump for a good ten, fifteen seconds when suddenly he grabs me and is like, "Oh my God, *Oh my God.* . . . The condom broke!" And I get off him, *fast.* I'm freaking out a bit and I'm like, "Oh my God, what? How do you *know?*" And he takes it off, examining it, and he's like, "Well, it's all wet down there." I lift my eyes, red and puffy from the pot, defeated and full of shame as I realize . . . "Oh. Well, that was me."

So, I guess it's safe to say that the whole experiment was basically a failure.

You'll be happy to know that Jon has accepted his homosexuality and hasn't had sex with a woman since. In fact he called me recently to tell me that he still has nightmares about that fateful day. I take it as a compliment. After all, I may not be able to turn a gay man straight, but I do leave a fellow with an experience he'll never forget.

CHAPTER 9

KINK ABOUT IT

oh my God, what have you domme!?

Different strokes for different folks, so the adage goes. The type of stroke that gets you stoked can come from a hand or a spiked paddle. There are many ways to deviate from the norm, and sometimes pleasure is a real pain. Submit to your desires, but master your impulses! Here's a little of the "he sade, she sade" about what happens when you indulge in sex with a twist. The lesson here: Don't be the party pooper at a fetish fête . . . unless you're into that kind of thing.

RED

by Will McLaughlin

I went to see a dominatrix—twice. I discovered my dominatrix online by accident.

Most of the dominatrix Web sites looked like the work of children who had just learned HTML: overly saturated backgrounds, misaligned photos, clip art. Horrid. Then I saw the link for "Mistress Duress . . . A sublime and versatile lifestyle domme." Sublime and versatile lifestyle—just like the West Elm catalog.

Mistress Duress appeared to have all the qualities I look for in a woman: tall, blonde, large-breasted, tasteful use of Flash animation. Moody Sigur Rós-esque ambient music rolled gently in the background as I clicked through pictures of her in latex nurse uniforms, cinching up men's genitals in horrible rope prisons. I'd like to meet this woman, thought I. I called the number and booked an appointment. For anthropological reasons. Just to find out if I was that type of person. It's very hard to broach the topic with a girlfriend. So I was thinking, tonight, after we go see *The Notebook*, maybe you could tie me to your bed and flick nickels at my balls.

My first anthropological finding was that this business is very secretive. I booked a 3 p.m. appointment. They told me to be at the corner of Twenty-third Street and Eighth Avenue. They would reveal the actual address five minutes before my appointment. Very strange. But I complied. Five minutes before my appointment, I was given an Eighth Avenue address just a stone's throw from the Upright Citizens Brigade Theatre in New York.

I made my way to the second floor of a typical New York City brownstone. I entered. And where a living room with a futon would normally be was a dark "lobby" with a large-breasted Latina woman sitting at a high desk. She was the only one in the room. I explained who I was, and she gave me a clipboard and sent me into the "Red Room." I was instructed to sit on the edge of the bed and fill out the form.

When I opened the door to the Red Room, here's what I saw: to my left, a large, wooden four-poster bed painted black with black vinyl cushions; in front of me, a cylindrical glass case that used to hold desserts in a diner and now displayed ball gags, butt plugs, and other arcana; to my right, a small folding table with a bowl in the middle containing fun-size servings of Twix, KIT KATS, and Wrigley's Chewing Gum.

I sat on the edge of the bed and began to fill out my form. It was a letter-size page with empty boxes and descriptions of fetishes next to them. I was to put a check by the things that I definitely did not want to explore. Right off the bat, I checked off forced homosexuality, piercing, bleeding, cross-dressing, and infantilism. No, thank you. I didn't have an interest in many of the things on the list. But I had kind of a chip on my shoulder at this point. For instance, a "Brown Shower" was being shat upon. I had absolutely no interest in being shat upon. But part of me wanted to see if this mistress could shit on command.

As I finished ticking off all my boxes, Mistress Duress entered. She looked just like her pictures: statuesque, tall in stiletto heels, clad in black vinyl and fishnet stockings. Awesome. Then she spoke. It was like Kathleen Turner had swallowed Greta Garbo and Ellen Barkin and they were having a pillow fight. She asked me some background questions, presumably because I looked like a cop. She asked for my fetish sheet and for the "contribution" of two hundred dollars. She said, "I'm going to leave the room now and study your sheet. You are to disrobe and sit at the edge of the bed to wait for my return. When I return, the scene will begin. If at any point you are not comfortable with the way the scene is going, the safety word is 'red.' Try as hard as you can not to say it, though. Only use the word 'red' if we are exploring an area you are uncomfortable with. This is a safe space. And please wear those flip-flops. No bare feet are allowed."

I was very nervous and excited. I was naked on the edge of the bed. Half my genitals were inside me at this point. She re-entered in the same outfit. The first thing Mistress Duress had me do was assume the position called "Bitch Boy," in which I lay on my back with my legs in the air and presented my ass to her. The second position was "Slut Boy," in which I presented my ass to her, doggy style.

I started to get scared. I have never had anything in my ass before other than an errant finger during a blowjob. But we did learn a lot about my ass that day. Chiefly that my sphincter muscle is stronger than the Great Wall of China. Mistress Duress attempted to penetrate me with a finger, and my ass, having spent a lifetime expelling matter, promptly kicked her out. I was all reflex. Which is when she went to the cabinet. While in Slut Boy position, Mistress Duress inserted a small vibrating egg into my ass and turned it on. It was a weird sensation that, I'm a bit ashamed to admit, was not entirely unpleasant. She then began to whip me with a cat-o'-nine-tails so that I would begin to associate pleasure (egg) with pain (whip). Smart, I thought.

After a while, she stopped the flogging and forced me to chase after her with my mouth. She made me worship her breasts, vagina, and ass. This was more my speed. Then she made me masturbate into my own hand, and before I knew it, the session was over.

Kind of bullshit.

I mulled over my experience for a couple of weeks. Is that what BDSM is? Was she just pulling punches because it was my first time? Did my asshole fuck things up for me? The questions raged. A month later, I made another appointment.

Same drill. But when I entered, I saw a young, beautiful brunette girl lighting candles in the lobby. My goodness.

I didn't have to fill out a form this time, though, because I was on file. Mistress Duress entered and looked at me quizzically. "Sally (the receptionist) says that you've been here before? I don't remember you." Well, fuck me. Sorry, but I'm on file. "I'll go look at your file and then we'll begin the scene. Also, I should mention that Mistress Mynx is also here today. And she could be in this session for a contribution of two hundred dollars more." *Two women!* This was fantastic! The candle girl in the lobby must have been her.

I sat naked and vulnerable on the edge of the bed. Mistress Duress walked in as beautiful and statuesque as ever. Followed closely by Mistress Mynx . . . who was not the beautiful brunette from the lobby, but a haggard, pock-marked, faded jailhouse tattoo of a woman who looked like a centerfold from *Easyriders* magazine. My genitals sank further into my body. I wanted to call it off, but I thought I would hurt her feelings. And I didn't want to do that.

Again, it started with basic ass play bullshit. Honestly, how many times can you be hit in the ass and have it be exciting? They then escorted me over to a strange chair that separated my legs individually. They put an inflatable blindfold over my eyes and pumped it full of air so that I could see nothing.

As I sat in the chair, blindfolded, Mistress Duress gave me instruction. "Now, slave, we're going to find out if you can . . . Wait a minute. Mistress Mynx, where are the long ropes? . . . Oh. I thought we only needed the short ones because they only go through the top here. . . . Yes, but we also need the long ones because they all tie together around the bottom. . . . Ooh. I see. Sorry. . . . No problem. This *slave* knows it's all his fault anyway. Don't you, slave?" Yes. It's all my fault you don't have the right ropes. How thoughtless of me. "Now that you're tied down, slave, you'll be at . . . okay, where is the long extension cord? . . . Unnnhh. I gave it to Sally earlier to use for her pencil sharpener. . . . Well, we're going to need it. Sally, could you do us a favor and bring in the long extension cord? . . . I'll be right there . . . Here you go, Mistress. Sorry about that. . . . Oh, it's okay. This slave knows that it's all his fault. Don't you, slave?" Yes. It is totally my fault that you don't have your shit together. Anyway, once they got their logistics straight, they had some sort of Tesla coil–like device that allowed them to electrify their hands as they grabbed my genitals. Interesting. They unchaired me and took me back to the bed to engage in foot worship—an area in which I excel.

Mistress Duress and Mistress Mynx lay down on the bed as I worshipped both of their feet using my hands and mouth. They began to chat. Mistress Mynx started the conversation. "So, have you decided what you're going to do with the other room? . . . Yes. I want to paint it gold. Like metallic gold. And I want to do a whole wall in mirrors. But not just glass. You see how those mirrors have those neat edges? . . . Yeah. It's called a beveled edge. . . . Right. I want to get a bunch of those because I like that effect where the edges meet. But I want to get a bunch of different kinds. . . . Well, I should introduce you to my friend Robert. Do you know the mirror over the bar in Balthazar? . . . Yes! I love that mirror. . . . Well, Robert bought most of the glass for that. He goes antiquing all over New England and finds the coolest things. . . . Oh, that would be great. I'd love it if he could find me. . . ."

I screamed, *"Red!!!"* What did you say, slave? "You heard me. . . . I said *red!*"

I marched over to my clothes and started jamming them back onto my body, only then realizing that my ass crack was still full of Vaseline. Mistress Duress asked Mistress Mynx to leave the room. "Are you okay? What went wrong?" What went wrong? Are you fucking kidding me? You don't have the right goddamn ropes. Your Tesla coil extension cord is being used for a pencil sharpener in the lobby. And now I'm down here working my ass off on both of your feet and you two are gabbing away like you're at brunch. *Red!* "I know. I'm

sorry. Look, I'm just training her right now. It's her first day."
I sensed she was about to weep. I tried to console her in my
rage. "Hey, look. You're awesome. She's horrible. And when
you two are together, she only brings you down." She nodded
as if she knew. "Look. I won't charge you for Mistress Mynx."
Good! 'Cause I wasn't paying for her. "I want to make this
up to you. We have a lot of parties that are invitation only.
You usually have to be a regular to get invited. But I want to
invite you to make sure you have a good experience. Would
that be okay with you?" I don't know. I guess. "Okay. I'll be
right back."

I can't say whether it was my perception of my power at
the time or if it was actually, physically true. But it appeared
that Mistress Duress has slipped out of her skyscraper stilet-
tos and was standing flat on the floor. She looked like a petite
little girl who came up to my chin. "Do you want to take a
shower? Or do you want to hang out and have a beer or something? It's on the house." No, thanks. She gave me a card with
a special access code for the party invite section of her Web
site. And then she gave me a disappointed kiss on the lips
as I stormed out the door. As a final act of defiance, I ripped
up the card on the way down the stairs. In a fit of malice, I
tossed the pieces onto the doorstep. I thought it over and realized that was a dick move. I carefully picked up the pieces
and threw them in a nearby trash can.

Moral of the story: You can whip me. You can degrade me.
You can electrify my genitals with a Tesla coil. But do not
fucking ignore me.

FOOT SLAVE

by Michael Feldman

When hearing the word "foot" one thinks, walking, shoes, smelly . . . but some among us hear "foot" and think, I want to fuck that.

I met Steve at a coffee shop in San Francisco a few years ago. We went through the usual flirtatious routine: glimpses in each other's direction, followed by long stares, followed by actually talking to each other. I gave him my number, and that night he called me because he really enjoyed meeting me. He felt he could be totally honest with me about what he likes. I thought he was going to say something endearing like "nerdy Jews who wear their glasses crooked." Instead he said, "I like feet."

He asked, "Do you like your feet massaged?"

"Yes!" I said. "Foot massages are awesome!"

"Do you like your feet licked?"

"Sure."

"So would you like it if we were hanging out, and you can be sitting on the couch, watching TV, and I can be your footstool . . ."

". . . Uhhhh . . . what?"

"Like, I'll be on all fours, and you'll put your feet on my back, like I'm your footstool. How does that sound?"

I wasn't sure how to respond. No one's ever asked to be my footstool before. *Then* he said, "I would love to be your slave. . . . Is there an aspect of your personality that likes this?" No. I don't deal well with high status. I'm known in many circles as the "I'm so sorry it was my fault" guy. Besides, as soon as he said "slave," I couldn't get the image out of my head of the pharaoh in ancient Egypt ordering all the Jews around to do his bidding. I had no desire to treat him as my ancestors were treated long ago.

"Well," I said, "when I first meet someone, I'm pretty shy and submissive myself."

"That's totally okay; I'd love to teach you. Do you mind if I call you a name, like 'Sir'? Or, 'Master'?"

". . . Sure."

"Okay, sir. Can you please call me a name?"

"Steve."

"No, not my real name, a *slave* name."

I bit my tongue hard not to say, "Kunta Kinte." "How 'bout 'Foot Slave'?"

"I like that."

He asked repeatedly if I looked down on him. My humble upbringing and taking up of Buddhism the past couple of years had taught me that I am no better, nor worse, than anyone. Even if I'm using you as my footstool, we are equals. So naturally I kept telling him that I didn't look down on him. Frustration peeking through, he said, "I really get off on people thinking they're better than me. Do you think you're better than me?"

Noooow I see where this is going—we're role playing! Which always seemed silly to me. If you're being that intimate with someone, I'd rather just call it out. Like instead of someone saying, "Hello, Sailor," I'd rather he say, "Hello,

Michael Feldman wearing a sailor outfit that he bought on eBay."

I placed my nonjudgmental spirit aside and played along: "Yes. I think I'm better than you, a little bit."

He asked, "If you were lying on a table nude and I could do anything to you, what would it be?"

"Hmm . . . massage my whole body?"

"Great, great, what else?"

"Uh . . . kiss and lick me all over."

"Great, great, what else?"

I didn't know what else to say, so he said, "Well, what about if I did your laundry for you?"

". . . What?"

"Yeah, ya know, I could do your laundry for you, I can clean for you. Does that turn you on?"

Again, I responded very honestly. ". . . Actually my mom does my laundry for me, so it's kind of detached for me sexually."

This honesty is why I'm not successful at phone sex. My one time having phone sex, it was winter in New York. I told the guy I was wearing baggy, gray sweatpants. He asked me to take them off and I said no. He thought I was teasing and playing hard to get, but I informed him that we have to pay for heat here so it's pretty cold in the apartment and I'd rather leave the pants on. I'm pretty sure he didn't come during our conversation.

So I wasn't sure Foot Slave was right for me, but he told me to think about it and get back to him. I was staying with my friend Gina and I told her everything. I had so many questions. Should I go over there? Should I be alone with him? What do I wear? Should I bring my laundry? She said, "You have to go, you're a writer, it'd be insane not to go." She was right. I was going on an adventure! I told her I would text her if I was getting murdered, and I was off.

On the way over to Foot Slave's house, he explained his philosophy to me:

"I want to go against the stereotype of what a man is. A man doesn't grovel at someone's feet, a man isn't a footstool. That's degrading. I like to hear that I'm a loser, get it out in the open, 'cause it's true."

Wow! I thought. We have *so* much in common.

We got to his place. He grabbed my hand, kissed it, and gave me the most adorable yet awkward five-second piggy-back ride to the couch. This is really nice, I thought. This night may actually be romantic.

He lay down on the ground next to my feet and began *licking my sneakers,* which totally surprised me. "Whoa!" I said. "Those are my shoes!"

"Does this make you uncomfortable?"

It dawned on me that he meant to lick my shoes, which indeed made me very uncomfortable.

"Let me show you how okay I am with this," he says and proceeds to lick my shoes more aggressively. This was not proving anything to me, and was making me feel nauseous. You do *not* know where those have been! blared in my mind. I tried wooing him with the promise of what was hiding inside the shoe: "My eleven-and-a-half-inch foot is ready to come out and play. Don't you like that? Feet? Ya know, without the shoes?" He explained that it's like a present on Christmas morning. You don't want it unwrapped right away; you want to play with it in the box for a while. His logic was severely flawed, as I truly didn't know anybody who wanted to do that. But rather than risk making him feel uncomfortable, I continued to allow him to lick my dirty sneakers.

Finally he took my shoes and socks off and started ecstatically barking like a dog. One of the many things I learned from this experience is that barking like a dog is very unattractive to me. To this day, I still get turned off whenever I hear a dog bark.

He continued worshipping my feet. "You're my master, my God. I could do anything for you, anything you want, just say it."

"Bring me a glass of water."

"Ice or no ice?"

"Ice."

"Crawl or walk?"

"Walking's fine!" I was drunk with power.

"Here you are, Master. I'm pathetic, right?"

"Yeah, a little bit."

"I'm a loser, right?"

"Yeah, a little bit."

"You can call me a loser. I'm below you, I'm nothing, right?"

"Yes, yes you are, a little bit."

His face completely transformed, like we were on a set and someone had just yelled, "*Cut!*" "Can you do me a favor? Can you not say 'a little bit'? Can you just say yes? Like, 'Yes, you are nothing; yes, you are a loser'? Okay?"

Later, when I related this to Gina, she mentioned that

saying "a little bit" was probably too honest. After all, really getting into the whole game of it is rough and sexual: Am I a loser? Yes, you are a filthy, dirty loser! It doesn't really work when you say, "Am I a loser?" "Hmmm . . . a little bit. . . ."

So, I apologized profusely to my slave, and next time I agreed to his demands.

He continued, "It's just me and you. What do you want me to do?"

This time I had more confidence: "Bring me another glass of water! No ice! And walk again!!"

He brought me the water, saying, "I'm pathetic. I'm gay and I'm ugly and fat and I'm nothing."

Again I responded way too honestly: "You're not fat."

He asked me to sit on his face and fart, which was hard 'cause I wasn't gassy. So I sat on his face and lied, "You feel that? Silent but deadly." Marking the first time a person has lied about farting when they actually *didn't* fart.

Suddenly I sensed impending doom. Oh shit, I thought, he's going to cut me up into little pieces and put me into his freezer. I wondered if I could order him not to kill me, but I thought that might be weird for him. And I didn't want to give him any ideas if he wasn't thinking about that to begin with.

I came to the conclusion that I really wanted to go home, so I demanded that my Foot Slave come. He looked surprised at first. "You want me to come now?"

"Yes."

"Right now?"

"Yes. Come now! Please! Just come!"

He came in his pants, and we kinda just sat there for a few

moments. You could cut the dissatisfaction with a knife. My Foot Slave transformed back into Steve. He said he should take me home because he had a "thing" in the morning.

For most of the car ride we barely looked at each other. We silently realized that we had made a huge mistake. I felt very disappointed in myself. Here's this guy who was willing to do *anything* for me! Anything I wanted. And I asked him for two ice waters. How could I waste such a wonderful opportunity?

Only one thing was certain: My mom was still going to have to do my laundry for me.

I was the real loser that night . . . a little bit.

CHAPTER 10

NEAR-DEATH SEXPERIENCES

the physical consequences of getting physical

When properly executed, intercourse should not land you in the hospital (unless it's a well-planned nine months later). For some, basic instincts trump survival instincts and can lead to injurious events. Sidestep these hazards of the hot and heavy, and avoid becoming a casual sex casualty. Beware of foreign objects, and trust your fight-or-flight response. Written in homage to the literal meaning of the cliché that love hurts, these bloody valentines will have you in stitches.

POKÉ-PON

by Boti Bliss

My friends, before I begin telling my action-packed adventure, I just want you to know: I have a new gynecologist!

Now let me set the scene:

The decade is the nineties. The city is Los Angeles. I'm not a girl, not yet a woman, clutching onto a waning childlike essence with a head of pink hair and a religious devotion to cartoons, the anime adventures of that yellow mouse-on-acid Pikachu of Pokémon fame topping the list.

Our story actually begins on a second date—the first one ending with some fantastic above-the-waist action and only a few "I'm not that kind of girl" remarks, which he courteously obeyed.

This time I actually ask him out and tell him it's my treat, the logic being if I pay for dinner I can therefore refuse sex without feeling pressured or guilty. Besides, our wonder date will be chaperoned by my monthly visit from Aunt Flow. This is actually fine, as I am not a big fan of sex during this time, even when it involves total darkness and the laying down of protective towels. Yes, I know it has been done in the history of sex, but never on the second date. And like I said, I am not that kind of girl.

So, it's date night, I'm gussied up to the nines, and feeling the effects of a glass of chardonnay, I impulsively decide just before heading out the door to do something I had never done before. In a flashback to my dance company days, I remember some time-honored advice for those who find themselves both on the rag and in a skimpy outfit: Cut off the tampon string. When one is executing a flying grand jeté, one wants the audience's attention to be on technique and not twat plugs. Not that I plan on doing any flying leaps, but with the way my dates go, one never knows. So, I implement this trick— a strange choice, I know, but lets remember we are talking about a girl who is taking her cues from poorly translated Japanese anime:

"Must cut cotton crotch-plug string for maximum Happy Sexy Power!"

Cut to the dinner that I can't afford but am going to pay for so I don't have to have sex. It starts with a martini . . . or two, then wine, and somewhere halfway through the second bottle I find myself completely and utterly socks-off charmed by this guy. He's making me laugh like I've never laughed before, entertaining me with the most amazing stories that I am really and genuinely pretending to listen to. His lips are moving, but I'm not hearing a word. I just keep nodding and thinking, This guy is stealing my heart right out of my chest! He . . . he just may be my soul mate! I am *sooooo* . . . gonna fuck him! Yes! Definitely gonna fuck him. *Tonight!* 'Cause as it turns out, I *am* that kind of girl.

I pay the bill and head to the powder room to regroup. In the stall—where I call upon the powers of my own Pokémon of Prudence and Anti-Sluttiness—I realize that my red tide has receded. It's surely a sign from above! Like the miraculous parting of the Red Sea, I was being granted permission to let my Moses pass through!

We get into his car and no sooner has he tipped the valet than my face is in his crotch. He somehow manages to Dale Earnhardt Jr. our way safely off Sunset Boulevard and into an empty parking lot. I don't know how many of you have actually had sports-car sex, but it's challenging! It takes great focus and determination and all sorts of inventive contortions. I had to—like my dear Pokémons—undergo metamorphosis and transform myself into a similar but stronger species. 'Cause nothing—and I mean nothing—was going to stop me.

I went to his place that night and found myself still there a few days later. It's a new relationship, so we're fucking like every ten minutes. Total bliss. Until one morning I wake up not feeling so good. I can't explain it; I just don't feel quite right . . . all over. Seeing that a new guy has been recently introduced to my puss-puss, I decide to visit my gynecologist. I get in the straps; she digs around, takes the tests . . . and nothing. They all come back negative.

So, I go back to his place and make him take care of me for a week and a half while I lay in bed watching Pokémon cartoons. Hey, that dinner I paid for was expensive *and* I put out! He owed me.

That night he draws me a bath. As I get out of the tub, I catch a glimpse of myself in the mirror. The veins in my arms and legs are glow-in-the-dark electric blue—I'm a fucking neon sign! I start to panic and I feel like I am going to faint and just then the contractions kick in. I feel like somebody is stabbing me in the ovaries. I am thinking, What the fuck? What the fuck? Am I having a baby or some shit? I manage to sit down on the commode and *plop* . . . something falls out! I go in for a closer look.

As it turns out, tampon strings are there for a reason.

I cannot begin to describe my feelings of horror that something basically resembling a not yet fully developed, bluish, reddish, slightly yellowish, slimy, cocooned mouse fetus had just fallen out of my vagina.

I had hatched my own little Poké-pon.

I reach out to flush it down and put it out of its misery, but seeing that it's ten times the size of a dead goldfish, I suddenly feel like I am committing some kind of murder. I debate scooping it up and putting it in a jar of formaldehyde, but where would I get formaldehyde, and how would I ever get it past my new guy, who is now frantically banging on the door, saying he heard screams, and asking, "Is everything okay?"

The doorknob slowly begins turning, and I am faced with a panicked choice: the man, or the Poké-pon?

Ladies and gentlemen, I am happy to tell you, I went against the advice of the English-dubbed Pikachu devil sitting atop my shoulder and flushed that rascal down. Because even though I got myself a bad case of toxic crotch, nine and a half years later, I still have the man!

I GOT HER NUMBER, SHE GOT MY DIGIT

by Drew DiFonzo Marks

I found a journal entry that I had written right before senior year of high school. It read:

Drew, here are three goals for senior year.

1: Throw an awesome party. Like the ones in the movies.

2: Be more like Ferris Bueller.

3: Ask out Jamie Wilcox.

Jamie Wilcox had been a crush of mine for years. She was all the clichés: smart, beautiful, made me feel like the world was in slow motion when she walked down the halls. I mainly knew her through the drama club. She was two things in our drama club: always the leading lady and, more importantly, the director's daughter.

Unlike everything you think of when you hear the phrase "drama club director," Mr. Wilcox was a very large and intimidating man. We used to say that if you ever forgot a line, Mr. Wilcox would pull out his six-foot-long dick, wrap it around your throat, and get an erection when you said the line correctly, thus making your head pop off and killing you instantly.

I, like everyone else, was terrified of Mr. Wilcox.

Currently we were doing a production of *Twelfth Night* that had brilliantly been adapted so that Duke Orsino was the producer of a record company. At the closing night cast party I found myself alone with Jamie, one thing led to another, and we kissed.

Slowly but surely Jamie became my high school sweetheart; however, this was a secret romance. Mr. Wilcox could
never know—in his mind Jamie was a virgin princess perched
atop a tower that nobody would ever be able to climb, and if
you ever tried he'd rip you to pieces with his bare hands. So
all of our encounters were kept off the radar; we made sure
we always covered our tracks so he would never know.

One day Jamie and I cut class and had sex in her bedroom. This was good sex, wild sex, passionate sex. . . . They say
the average male reaches his sexual peak at age eighteen. I
believe it. This was the kind of sex that leaves scratch marks
and causes damages that cost money to repair. During this
frenzy one of the many things we knocked over was the phone.

You know that weird moment when you pick up the phone
and somebody is already there on the other end, because they
called you right at the moment you picked it up?

Mr. Wilcox had called home, trying to leave a message
about leaving the chicken out to thaw or God knows what,
and instead heard his princess daughter getting the shit
fucked out of her.

Instead of hanging up immediately, Mr. Wilcox listened
in. And he listened good. Unbeknownst to me, Mr. Wilcox for
some time now had suspected his wife of having an affair,
and he thought he'd caught her in the act. He was on the
hunt, straining his ears for any clue as to who this bastard
was. Eventually I made his detective work easy for him by
screaming something along the lines of "Fuck it, Jamie, I'm
coming on your face." It was high school, we were in love,
that's what you do.

After some brief cleanup, Jamie put the phone back on the hook, neither of us realizing what had happened. Immediately it rang. She answered. Mr. Wilcox was so loud that I could hear him from across the room when he said, "I heard everything. I'm on my way home. Tell Drew to stay where he is."

I was dead.

Thinking I was about to have my head ripped off by an insane man's gargantuan penis, I decided it was best to run. It was fight or flight, and every fiber of my being said, Fucking fly. I started throwing my clothes on, scrambling to find my socks, hoping that I could get in my car and drive away with my life. Jamie was moving just as frantically as I was. She ran into the bathroom, and I dove in behind her to grab my glasses, but she ended up slamming the door just as I was reaching out, catching my finger in the door hinge.

The door quickly closed on my finger, making a thick crunching sound. I tried but could not get it out. I howled in pain. I felt the door loosen up and I thought, Oh, thank God this pain is over, only to feel the door slam hard again, and then again. Over and over the door slammed, crushing my finger to pieces with it. Jamie couldn't hear my screaming over the music, and she thought a towel was caught in the door. Blood poured down the white walls, I couldn't get my hand out, and I was about to black out from the pain.

The door finally swung open. I fell to the ground clutching my hand, feeling blood spatter all around me. Jamie looked at me and said sweetly, "Oh, I'm sorry, baby, did I crunchy your finger in the door?" I opened my left hand to show her that I was holding my right index finger, completely severed.

She screamed. I screamed. I blacked out.

The ER was able to sew it back on.

The next day back at school, with a huge bandage on my right hand keeping my finger attached, I had an after-school drama club meeting. I knew for certain that today was the day I would die. I sat as close to as many other students as I could, hoping that when Mr. Wilcox came in, guns blazing, I could use them as human shields or at least to subdue his weaponized hard-on. I knew my evasive maneuvers wouldn't save me, however, when the door at the back of the auditorium was kicked in violently, revealing the silhouette of Mr. Wilcox. Somehow he managed to make a brightly lit auditorium feel like a dark Western saloon just with the use of his foot. He screamed, *"Drew! Come Here!"* I slowly walked up to him, knowing that all my friends behind me were about to witness a murder, but was sure that none of them would testify, for they were all smarter than me and knew to never cross Mr. Wilcox.

Wilcox looked down at me. Put his arm around my neck. Squeezed tightly. Looked me in the eyes and said, "Well, you're one of the family now."

CHAPTER 11

ON THE REBOUND

the art of getting back in—and—out there

*Much has been said about the best way to get over a lost love.
Throw yourself into your work. Take up a new hobby. Focus
on yourself. Or take the bold approach and just have sex with
someone else, and quick. Compromise your standards, quiet
your conscience, find a liberator, and embrace your freedom.
The almighty rebound lay can be effective in getting you back in
the game, as long as nobody plays dirty. Here we encounter
some brokenhearted souls that decided to test the old theory:
In order to get over one, you must get under many.*

MODEL BEHAVIOR

by Eric W. Pearson

Our civilization sustains itself on various theories and principles, one of which states that all things, good and evil, joyous and tragic, sweet and bitter, will eventually balance out. In support of this theory I propose to you the account of how an eventually beneficial yet heart-wrenching breakup balanced itself out when a once-in-a-lifetime opportunity to triumph turned into a floundering calamity laced with fear and shame.

So Tara dumped me. It wasn't even a surprise. I saw the messy end coming from months away, but I just couldn't stop being really into her. Logic screamed in my ears that the relationship would end and that if anyone was going to be devastated by it, it was going to be me. I should have listened, but instead I called her too much, complimented every single outfit she wore, and did everything I could to establish myself as a subordinate until my last dying soldier pitifully waved the white flag.

Tara and I only bumped uglies for seven months, but the rejection caused me an irrational and unreasonable amount of suffering. I transformed from a casual smoker into a chimney. Food tasted shitty. Jokes weren't funny. Things just sucked, and I was consciously amazed by how much things sucked. The break happened right before Thanksgiving and maintained momentum until a few days after Christmas, when I flew from Boston to Los Angeles.

Men always seem to meet insultingly beautiful girls when they are in a situation to do nothing about it, and in my case, I met a professional model named Carina on that flight back to LA. Carina crushed any foolish notion of our hooking up by mentioning her fiancé, a financial whiz kid who had retired at the age of twenty-four. I thought nothing of it when we exchanged phone numbers upon our arrival at LAX.

On a Tuesday evening about two weeks later I had planned to go out with some friends. Maybe a half hour before everyone was meeting at my place I got a phone call. It was Carina.

"It's my birthday. I just got out of dinner, and I don't want to go home. What are we going to do?" From that moment I sweated on and off for the rest of the night.

Carina offered to drive my friend Lindsey and me to the club that we were going to. Carina's intoxication became clear as day when she ran through a stop sign, almost causing a serious collision, and popped a curb *hard* while turning into the parking garage. By the time we got out of the car Lindsey's hands were visibly trembling.

Once inside the club, Carina asked if we wanted to sit down. Looking around, I could see that every booth was already jammed with people, and I tried to explain this to her. Her response:

"I'll be right back."

A few moments passed as I felt the judgmental yet amused stares from my friends, and then I saw Carina waving us to the front of the club where she had sweet-talked a group into basically giving up their booth for us.

Once again I had underestimated the power of the pretty.

The earlier drunken death ride and the numerous cigarettes I'd already smoked in a futile attempt to calm myself
had made me a vibrating ball of nerves. Tragic as it was, I
had to excuse myself from the booth to take a shit in this
chichi-assed place.

After sharing a good-hearted chuckle with the bathroom
attendant who thought my predicament was "fuckin' funny,
maing," I came back to find Carina dancing. And boy, was
she dancing. She was doing this twirling move that sent her
long skirt into orbit and put her taut undercarriage on display for every man, woman, and busboy to see. I felt like I
had to shit again.

My friends were getting far too much entertainment
from her performance, so I grabbed Carina and suggested
we take a cigarette break. Unfortunately, the route to the
smoking area brought us past a little problem called the bar.
I couldn't stop her from ordering a drink and then berating
the bartender for never having heard of it before. It wasn't
clear if her ultimate goal was to get a drink or make this
poor guy feel bad. Either way, he saw that I was in over my
head and decided to fuck me over in the form of a free triple
Jäger shot.

After Carina inhaled the shot, we walked outside to
smoke. She bulldozed her way through a crowd to the ropes
separating official club territory from the outside world. I
followed as best I could, dealing with all the pissed off people who caught elbows or shoulders from her. By the time
I reached Carina there were about a dozen people demand-
ing an explanation from me about her. Luckily, she explained

it all by hopping the ropes and falling flat on her face. The crowd laughed their asses off.

Carina finished a business card transaction with, of all people, the owner of a dance studio who wanted her to come by and cut a rug, and we moved a few feet away from the ropes and lit two cigarettes. I started to ask her what presents she got for her birthday when she kissed me. Hard. To the point. This quickly transitioned to her stretching out the collar of my shirt and hungrily devouring my upper sternum.

In general, hardcore public displays of affection embarrass me. That, combined with the utter lack of power I had in this situation, made me very embarrassed very quickly. On top of that I had left my friend Lindsey in the club with two people she didn't know at all. I had to get back inside.

We hadn't been sitting in the booth for more than one full minute before Carina pounced on me, French-kissing me with extra French. I had to get out of this situation, or at least the public aspect of it, and reassess. After apologizing profusely to my friends, I escorted Carina out.

Total time spent in the club? Thirty-five minutes, and that's being generous.

As we rode the escalator down to the parking garage I heard her leave a message for her fiancé, telling him that she was going to stay at her friend's place for the night. It was around this time that I discovered it wasn't just her birthday, but also the day that she had moved in with the guy she was going to marry. Watching her leave that message felt like receiving a phone call from Satan to confirm my reservation in hell.

By the time I drove us back to my apartment, my pit stains had reached heroic proportions. Inside, I gave her my cigarettes, a lighter, and a glass of water, and told her to meet me on the balcony. I went to the bathroom for the old water-on-the-face, stare-in-the-mirror cliché. Can I do this? A soon-to-be-married woman? A clearly intoxicated woman? I really shouldn't. I wonder if things would have played out differently if I had known then that I would have no choice.

I checked the balcony. Empty. I checked my bedroom. There she was. There she was, no longer wearing a shirt. There she was, stumbling out of her skirt. There she was, cracking up at herself as she ripped some very complicated boots off her feet.

And there I was, looking white as a ghost and standing rigid as a Douglas fir.

Carina grabbed me and brought us down onto the bed like she was Dwayne "The Rock" Johnson. Her mouth dominated my mouth, and her hands were like greased lightning with my belt, then pants. As this was all going down, I realized that there was another problem.

My erection wasn't erect. Not . . . even . . . close.

Why, you may ask, would a young buck such as myself stay flaccid in the middle of such a common American male fantasy? I don't know, but I can speculate.

First, I was morally conflicted. Her fiancé sounded like a douchebag,* and he obviously did something pretty bad to make her ditch him on her birthday, but this was still his future wife angrily trying to access my wedding tackle. Second, my ex, Tara, almighty being that she was, still had authority in the dominion of my heart. Carina and I were in my bed, and I couldn't help but think that I'd had better times in this bed with a girl that I was more into and more comfortable with. Third, I was scared shitless. No question about it.

Carina, meanwhile, knew exactly what she wanted: me in her. Anticipating the humiliation of revealing my wilted flower, I did my best imitation of an assertive person by trying to go down on her. Between her legs, I found a bramble of untamed pubic hair. Oh, so girls like this don't shave or even trim? Makes sense.

I couldn't even make my first cunnilingus move before Carina pulled me up by my hair. It was foolish of me to think I was going to distract her by chowing box when she had already made up her mind on the aforementioned "me in her thing." It was also foolish of me to think that she'd realize she was trying to stuff a wet noodle into a hairy cup. She just kept trying harder. It was awful.

Finally I dismounted and lay down next to her. Carina: "What's wrong?"

Me: "I'm not sure if we should do this." Carina stared my masculinity into a dark, sad corner.

Me: "It's just . . . I don't know. You have a fiancé. I can't help but think you want to do this as an act against him, and you don't really want me."

In any other situation her smile would have been the sexiest thing ever.

"I'll show you!"

To female readers, I apologize. It is very difficult to

explain the discomfort and anxiety that a man feels when a girl takes his limp penis into her mouth, commences a high-effort blowjob, and absolutely nothing happens. I'd like to say it is something like the nonmedical version of a gynecological exam, but honestly, how the fuck would I know? Regardless, it is no fun.

After spending too long down there, she surrendered. I looked at her lying next to me, very naked, and I found a morsel of satisfaction by theorizing that Carina had never in her life come this far to find the guy not ready and able to fuck her senseless. She looked confused, flabbergasted even. Regrettably, I think she saw it as a failure on her part, and henceforth doubled her efforts.

Time stood still, but I estimate that we spent about thirty minutes rolling around together. Carina still wanted sex, and she explored all possible paths. One of the more intense moments came when she thought, Maybe he's into pain. I had visible teeth marks (the full thirty-two) on my left biceps for over two weeks. For the most part I managed to control her upper body, keeping a majority of the action limited to kissing, which had been the best part for me thus far.

After the estimated half hour of her failed attempts to awake my unit, it appeared that she'd accepted her fate. We lay there together, naked and entangled, and talked. Laugh if you must, but it was really nice. In this state she was fun to talk to, and soon we were laughing and play-fighting and acting "cute" together.

The problem with this sudden pleasantness was that it made me comfortable, and being comfortable with her made the sun shine on my wilted flower. Without warning, it bloomed! That crafty bitch.

Somehow Carina realized that I had a boner before I did. Never let it be said that she is not a woman of quick, decisive action. I was still "acting cute together" when she dropped herself onto my cock, emitting an authoritative "I did it!" moan. By my definition (one full thrust) we had already had sex.

I was kind of freaked out, but thankful to know that I could still get erections. I decided to stop being the nice guy and accept the fact that I can't *not* have sex with this girl anymore despite all of my prior pathetically valiant efforts. I rotated our bodies so that she was on her back and I was on top. She responded well to this faint glimpse of confidence. I paused to drink in the entire scene, and just as I was about to execute my sexual game plan, I hear,

"Fuck me harder!"

Odd, I wasn't even fucking her at all when she said it, but now's not the time to split hairs. Now is the time to fuck hard. So I began to fuck her reasonably hard. I thought it was going well, but . . .

"You're going to have to fuck me harder than that."

Okay, I'm not normally in love with excessive, repetitive instructions, but I can still be into this. I turned up the speed and force of my thrusts, yet still heard

"Harder! Fuck me *harder!*"

Jesus Christ. Fine! I started fucking her literally as hard and as fast as I could. I was fucking her so hard that I wasn't even enjoying it. It sounded like a high-powered machine gun firing sirloin steaks at a heavy-duty trash bag. After five minutes of this (and that's being generous) I was exhausted. I was drenched in sweat, and droplets of said sweat were falling onto her. She was moaning and squealing, but the most common sound coming out of her mouth was

"Fuck me harder!" All of my best "harder, faster, stronger" efforts were only met by

"Harder! Harder! Fuck me harder!"

Finally I stopped what I was doing and said, "This is the hardest! It doesn't get any harder than this! You're obviously used to having sex with guys who are in *way* better shape than I am."

"Fuck me harder!"

God damn it.

I like to consider myself a logical person, and logic told me that I did not have the necessary tools to give her what she wanted. So like any other guy faced with this type of challenge, I gave up. I resumed having sex with her, but at my own pace. I did my best to drown out her barking orders, and focused on ending this my way. I even closed my eyes to focus on better things than this unbelievably hot model in my bed who was crying for more. God, that's depressing.

The sex ended with a whimper, not a roar. I lay down next to her. "Sorry that wasn't what you were looking for."

She forced a smile. "No, it was very nice."

Pause. "Don't bullshit me."

We laughed. At least we both had a sense of humor about my shortcomings. She traced her hand across my chest and said, "Know what I'd really like to do now?"

"What's that?" I was hoping it was get food.

"I really want to fuck you."

"But . . . We just . . . Carina . . . Didn't we . . . I thought . . .?"

"I want to fuck you *so* bad."

Holy fucking shit. Who is this girl, and what species is she?

I spent another twenty to thirty minutes fending her off. She bit me a few more times and tried the wet noodle/hairy cup game as well, but I was once again terrified and not about to let anything go down. Finally she fell asleep, and I mean out cold.

Once I knew she was asleep, I rushed out to my balcony to regain my sanity. Three cigarettes later I formed a plan where I would wake her, ask her what she wanted to do, and make sure I presented the option of calling her fiancé.

I couldn't even accomplish phase one. She was so very unconscious. Turning the lights on didn't wake her. Removing the comforter and sheets didn't wake her. Whispering "Carina" didn't wake her. Yelling "Carina" didn't wake her. An ice cube on her naked back didn't wake her. I gave up trying to wake her up when I lifted her arm up, let go, and her own falling hand slapped her across the face (pretty hard too).

I woke up the next morning to find her getting dressed. She turned to me and smiled before saying, "This wasn't a good idea."

I couldn't argue.

I walked her to her car and waved as she drove off. I called her later that day to make sure she had gotten home all right, but ended up leaving a message. I got no response.

I waited about a week and then sent her a text message to check in. The next day she responded via text message:

"Please don't call me anymore."

PS: I researched everything I could on Carina after this incident. While reading her interview in a magazine, I found two fascinating quotes.

"I've never had a one-night stand. . . . I'm a very no-sex-on-the-first-date type of person. It ruins things."

"Memo to men: Sex isn't over until both people get off."

SLEEPS WITH DOGS

by Jennifer Hirshlag

"Sleeps with Dogs"—that's what the slogan on the T-shirt read.

My revulsion toward this item was surely justified. The T-shirt cheapened one of my favorite quarterly pleasures, my Orvis dog catalog stocked with all manner of escapist canine extravagances, from tartan dog beds embroidered with names like Bailey and Dylan to mahogany doghouses for mannered breeds that you could imagine ruling expansive country households far from my decaying, cramped, and yardless Brooklyn apartment.

But as my eyes furtively darted from one line of descriptive merchandise copy to the next, absorbing every detail of the garment—it was made in combed cotton and was "sure to make me smile"—it occurred to me that I was the lowly customer to whom the retailers were peddling this tacky product.

See, I sleep with dogs. I have always done so, and was doing so with a handsome Italian greyhound named Byron when at the age of thirty-two, I found myself suddenly not sleeping with the man I had slept with for the last twelve years of my life.

At the time, I was grateful to have Byron in my bed, and it wasn't just the companionship my adored pet provided at all times (especially on cold lonely nights). It was also because I had transformed. As I went from a newly single woman sadly inept at handling promising suitors to a

going-on-several-years single woman all too skilled at picking up guys I knew would only serve as temporary dalliances,
the dog proved to be a boon to my love life.

For example, if I met a hunky beau and uttered any of
the following then-truthful statements to him—"I just ended
a long-term relationship," "I have two cats," "I am a vegetarian," and (this one I could never understand), "No, I don't get
the Harry Potter phenomenon"—I could guarantee it would
be just me and the pooch in between my sheets that evening.
On the other hand, if I said "I used to be a competitive gym-
nast," "I work in fashion," "Ha, I'm *sooooo* drunk," or, and this
seemed to be key, "I have a dog"—well, then, I could just get
ready for the call of the wild, if you know what I mean.

It was a surefire strategy, especially the time I met one of
my last affairs. "I have this really amazing dog," I mentioned
to the boy my girlfriends nicknamed Prefontaine (after his
close resemblance to Jared Leto in the film about the seven-
ties runner), and suddenly there I was, racing a marathon in
the sack.

I had sound judgment in those days, but masochistically
I often chose to ignore it. This was the case with Prefontaine.
First, I swore that I would never mess with a paramour more
than a decade younger than I, and Prefontaine was twelve
years my junior. Second, Prefontaine was a little bit off, as if
he had been struck by lightning, or the test subject of a scientific experiment gone awry, or kicked in the head by a horse
as a toddler and never told by his doting parents.

The daftness resulted in odder and odder behavior, as
what I expected would be a one-night stand turned into a

relationship of sorts with Prefontaine calling every few days and showing up unannounced on my doorstep all the way in Brooklyn with a boner rather than a bouquet of flowers every Sunday afternoon.

There were subtle quizzical things, things that would give me pause, make me wonder if maybe I hadn't heard him correctly, like when I asked, "Do you want me to cook you some dinner?" and he replied, "In the kitchen?"

Then there were more obviously strange things, things that would make me first think he was joking, only he wasn't, like when he enthused about meeting a celebrity on the street who had just gone through a well-publicized divorce, and he asked him nevertheless if the young woman he was with was his wife.

And finally there were things that were just so out there that I believed I had to have fallen asleep after a bout of our sweaty tumbling and dreamt them. For example, once he got out of bed just seconds after an orgasm—his, not mine—and started pacing, nude, semi-flaccid, and nervously fingering the hangers in my closet. Oh no, I thought, is he going to try on one of my outfits? To see if it would turn me on if he wore my Marc Jacobs dress? To see if I'm that kind of girl who likes to experiment? I pulled my blanket up to my eyes in fear until he emerged from his excavation with—of all things— my baton.

"What's this?" Prefontaine demanded.

"I was the captain of my high school majorette team," I explained.

He began clumsily twirling the baton, the thin and

glistening rod swooping dangerously close to his own. And when he felt he seemed to have gotten the hang of it, he looked up to me and asked, "Where do you think things are going with us?"

I went through one of the most devastating periods in my life after that. And it wasn't because Prefontaine stopped calling me and the Sunday visits waned. It was because my dog, my dearest Byron, my true bedmate, had suddenly fallen ill.

One day I awoke and he wasn't there, curled up on the backsides of my legs or nestled within the curve of my belly or snuggling his black muzzle into my neck. I called him and received no response. I got out of bed and found him tucked into a tiny ball on the couch. I made an appointment to visit the vet that day.

The vet initially assured me everything was fine, but I knew otherwise. And soon it was revealed that Byron had cancer, a fast cancer that took over his body within months. Toward the end I often carried him to bed, but I would always wake up alone, him having retreated to an isolated spot in the corner of the room where I imagined he was preparing to die.

I put him down on a crisp and sunny fall afternoon. I first walked him through Gramercy Park, then stopped with him to get a tea at a café, and then brought him to the animal clinic. I cried before, during, and after the procedure. I cried when I got home to my empty apartment and turned off all the lights and shut all the curtains. I cried when I picked up the phone call that I assumed was my mother checking in to make sure I was holding up okay.

"Mom?" I said, sniffling.

"Jen?" I heard on the other line.

"Yes, who is this?" It wasn't my mom.

It was Prefontaine. I hadn't heard from him in a long time. I wanted to hang up, but how could I? So I gathered myself together just enough to tell him it wasn't a good time to talk.

"Are you okay?" he asked.

"No, I'm not okay. I put my dog to sleep today."

"No," he retorted, and I wondered, Maybe he'll mutter something sweet, something that will make me happy I accidentally picked up his call, that will make me wish I would resume our frequent check-ins and Sunday visits. Maybe he'll mutter something that will make me realize he was actually normal.

But instead there was a pause—a long, seemingly thoughtful and seemingly saddened pause—and then the following: "Wow, I can hardly believe it. I mean, I had a threesome with that dog."

See, I do sleep with dogs, and I have always slept with dogs. But the thing is, I have never done *that* with a dog.

And I never will, I can reassure you as I type this in bed beside my two-year-old female whippet who shimmies her way in between my husband and I every night. But she, like all the others that preceded her and will follow her, knows that when the kisses and groping start, her place is anywhere but in the bed.

I sleep with dogs. And maybe, now that I am admitting that, I will go ahead and buy that T-shirt.

TWO HOUSEHOLDS,
ONE A'LACKING DIGNITY

by "Juliet"

I was fresh out of a breakup with my first love, with whom I had been living for five years. I felt confused, vulnerable, and overwhelmed by the prospect of being single, especially in Los Angeles. My cousin—we'll just call her "Benvolia"— explained that the solution was simple: I just needed to have sex with someone—*anyone*. A romantic at heart, I laughed the idea off and told her that wasn't my style.

Instead I decided to throw myself into my other true love: acting. I signed up for a three-day intensive Shakespeare workshop. I thought if anyone would know my pain, it would be the Bard. We spent the first day learning how to be "present" and connected to those around us, which meant walking around the stage, staring at one another, and stopping from time to time when you "felt something" with someone. As luck would have it, the first person I felt something enough to connect with was a devastatingly handsome circa-1996 Leonardo DiCaprio type. We stopped two feet from each other and stood face to face. We gazed into each other's eyes and saw our true essences, life experiences, and authentic souls. The moment passed and we moved on.

I immediately ruled him out because he probably had a girlfriend or wife—oh, but no wedding ring, I noticed; he was probably gay; he was an actor who looked like Leo, so he must be a douchebag.* But on the third day, when I saw him do a monologue from *Hamlet*, my feelings began to change. Be still, my heart, I thought, he can act. When he approached me and complimented my Juliet, I could tell something was there. We stood there like two tragic Shakespearean figures, basking in mutual validation. Okay, I convinced myself, maybe we should be friends. So when the workshop was over, I sent him a casual email saying we should grab coffee sometime. Not a date— way too soon for me. Plus, *I* don't ask guys out! This was just a friendly thing. When he called and suggested that we go to see Shakespeare in the Park with a picnic and wine, I was still confident that this was just a friendly meeting between two actors with a shared appreciation for Shakespearean tragedy.

I was a little freaked out when I pulled up to his house because it looked really nice, and I suddenly realized how little I knew about *Hamlet* (the man *or* the play). I sat in my car fearing his wife and kids would run out onto the porch and welcome me, or worse, his parents. Turns out he really was just a single guy, living in a great house that he bought. And remodeled himself. He was bored while completing a double major at the University of Chicago, so (naturally) he had taken up carpentry, which explained all the beautifully crafted furniture and ornate architectural detailing. He had a roommate, he said, who was out of town.

Okay, so he wasn't stupid or gay, so maybe he'd be sleazy and overconfident or even worse, nervous and insecure. Nope, he was none of those. He had the perfect balance of very romantic, somewhat bold moves along with a calm and genuine confidence that put me at ease. Of course, the bottle of wine helped do the trick too.

After the play we went back to his place and hung out on his balcony (handcrafted from recycled wood), complete with a bonsai garden and sandpit that ignited into a fireplace. We talked for hours about anything and everything. We were so open and truthful with one another it felt like we were discovering an even higher level of "presence" and "connection" than our acting teacher had ever imagined. Perhaps we could co-author her next volume.

As we finished our second bottle of wine, it finally dawned on me: This is a date. And . . . I really like this guy. And so the panic began to set in. I felt like Juliet—naïve, consumed with passion, and desperately wanting to bone. I hadn't been on the dating scene since I was nineteen. I knew putting out on the first date was not the best idea, but I couldn't even remember what you do before sex. My head was spinning as he led me to his hand-carved canopy bed—just like the one from the Leonardo DiCaprio movie. And then I heard the calming voice of my cousin:

"Just fuck someone!"

Well, I couldn't ask for a better opportunity. So I quit stalling and went for it. As soon as he sensed I was onboard, he stopped and said those six words no girl wants to hear after she's unzipped a guy's pants: "I have to tell you something." Now that I think about it, I guess the two words that followed were even worse: "I'm married."

Well, he did have a great sense of humor; that was the other thing I really liked about him, so I laughed and laughed because that was *hilarious!* And as I laughed hysterically, I noticed he wasn't. And then it hit me. Like the flashbacks on prime-time crime dramas, I remembered that while I was admiring the mosaic tiles in his guest bathroom, I had noticed a hairbrush with long brown hair in it, but I had naturally assumed that it must belong to his roommate . . . who must have long, brown, curly hair. And then there was the pair of matching silk Chinese bathrobes hanging on the door. Again, I thought maybe he and his roommate had similar tastes? And wait a second . . . what single guy really cultures his own yogurt? Of course! It all made sense now. This guy was perfect: smart, handsome, confident, compassionate, with a great sense of style and interior design. He was everything a woman wants, so naturally he was married to one! I wasn't Juliet . . . I was Helena!

He went on to explain that six months ago he and his wife had tried a threesome, which turned out not to be to their liking, but allowed his wife to realize that she liked women as well as men, so she proposed an open marriage. She was gone for the night but knew about his date with me and was okay with it. He had wanted to be up front with me but was scared I would run away; he understood if I was pissed off and wanted to go home, but said that he really wanted me to stay.

I lay there staring up at the canopy, feeling robbed of my opportunity to play out my very own Baz Luhrmann movie. I wanted to complete this necessary step in getting over my ex-boyfriend. I didn't want to wake up in my lonely apartment and return to my heartbroken life; I wanted to stay in the hand-carved canopy bed and wake up to the bonsai garden, and the freshly cultured yogurt, and the sand that catches on fire, and the mosaic-tiled bathroom!

That "marrièd," that one word "marrièd"
Hath slain ten thousand maidens' hearts
But O, it presses to my memory
Like damnèd guilty deeds to sinners' minds!

Lost and conflicted, I turned and looked into his eyes. And in that moment we did exactly as our Shakespeare teacher had taught us. We connected . . . in the present. I could almost hear Des'ree's "Kissing You" playing in the background. Suddenly, none of it mattered: his sixteen-year relationship with his wife, my Catholic prudish upbringing, either one of our morals—we were both in the present! I wanted my fantasy, and I was going to let myself have it. Clothes were off, things were going well, and finally we were about to do it when he looked into my eyes with such deep love and affection his whole body began to shake and . . . he lost his erection.

Woe is me.

This, again, was an experience I had never had, and he claimed the same. He seemed more perplexed than I was, explaining that in all the years with his wife and even in their "unsatisfying threesome" he had never had that problem.

Well, neither of us was a quitter. We were so committed to consummating this star-crossed union that we went to work for roughly four and a half hours. It wasn't easy. It was a lot of hard work. It was like a duel. It took serious strength, concentration, endurance, and sweat. Finally, his sleeping member awoke, and I was suddenly visited by memories of my ex-boyfriend. Out of nowhere, tears began to pour out of my eyes. I was too shocked to stifle them, and since we were so "connected" and "present" I couldn't have hidden the sudden emotion from him anyway. He stopped and patiently asked me what was wrong. Like the perfect compassionate, flaccid fantasy man that he was, he comforted me . . . and suddenly I heard the front door open. My mind raced. Maybe his neighbor was coming over to make sure everything was okay after hearing the four-and-a-half hour struggle, or the police, or an intruder, or Chris Hansen, or Father Laurence? I don't know! I couldn't come up with a logical explanation. Then I looked at his face and knew it was worse than all the possibilities I had desperately wished for. It was his wife. It was suddenly a matter of fight or flight, and I was 100 percent committed to fleeing. Lady Macbeth was on her way to the bedroom, and I was in grave danger. I scanned the room looking for the easiest exit, while he calmly put on his clothes and handed me my dress.

He had mentioned before that he thought I should meet his wife; that meeting her would alleviate my anxiety about getting involved with a married man. Right. Someone would have to drag me kicking and screaming to get me anywhere near this woman. The only thing that finally convinced me to follow him into the living room was the realization that my only alternative was to stay in the bedroom, where she would eventually enter and meet me . . . there . . . next to the bed.

So I casually stumbled into the living room in my slinky black dress, with my hair in a big after-sex poof, trying to find my equilibrium after being horizontal for over four hours. I smiled and introduced myself. She giggled nervously and shook my hand. She had started watching a movie, *Thank You for Smoking*. "Oh, I've never seen that," I blurted. "It's supposed to be really good." Awkward pause. Then, just when things couldn't get any more awkward, he suggested that I spend the night.

I wondered what exactly "spending the night" meant. Would he sleep in his bedroom with her, which is what she wanted, or on the couch with me, which is what I wanted, or all three of us in one bed with him in the middle, which was his brilliant idea? Well, I didn't know the protocol for open marriages, but I quickly learned that the slut who is dumb enough to sleep with the married guy sleeps alone on the couch. At this point any person in her right mind would play dead or just jam the dagger in her heart, but at that moment (still "in the present" with this guy) I chose to be completely pragmatic. I wasn't living a Shakespearean romance. I would come out of this alive, yeah, and alone. And I had an 8 a.m. call time the next morning that was less than ten minutes from his house, over an hour from my house . . . and that's without traffic. Two households, one tough decision: sleep on the couch while Mr. Flaccid Fantasy Man sleeps with his wife in the adjacent room and lose all remaining dignity, or go home and drive back in about five hours . . . in LA traffic.

Well, I hate traffic.

As I lay there curled up on the couch, I wondered if this was the healing experience my cousin had been thinking of. And I realized why Shakespeare didn't have Juliet fall for Hamlet. Juliet was a young, romantic, lovesick beauty. Hamlet was a self-indulgent ass.

CHAPTER 12

A SEXUAL JOURNEY

sometimes it's not about one moment,
but a lifetime of memories

A wise man on daytime television once said, "Like sands through the hourglass, so are the days of our lives." We agree. For some of us, choosing just one bad sexual experience is like sifting out a single grain of sand from a vast desert of disappointment. The stories in this chapter reflect on the bigger picture of bad sex—not just one fleeting, horrible moment, but a lifetime of failure. Consider this: If you can view a sexual life like an Aristotelian adventure and believe that "the whole is more than the sum of its parts" while subscribing to Winston Churchill's opinion that "courage is going from failure to failure without losing enthusiasm," then these authors should be viewed as courageous souls with large wholes.

"For a just man falleth seven times, and riseth again."
The Holy Bible

RUB-A-DUB-DUB,
THANKS FOR THE . . . NUB?

by Casey Wilson

Gentle reader. Some context: Some time ago a gentleman caller broke up with me and then in the same breath asked if he could fuck me in the ass. I obliged. So now we're all caught up!

It's time to move even further back in time, back when I was even stupider. Won't you come with me back in time?

No, not back to Connor, who demanded we listen to an obscure AM radio program on aliens while we had sex.

Further.

No, not the time my fellow loudly farted while teary-eyed we stood, literally on my late mother's grave—and fine, that's not sex, but I think it's worth mentioning, don't you?

Back further.

Was it the time my handsome boyfriend and I were sidled up to at an eighties dance club and asked by a bright-eyed young thing if we would care to go home with her? As I answered, "Um, I don't think—," I heard him say, "That could be cool. . . ."

Further back still.

I'm in my high school boyfriend's bed, and we are having sex when his mom unexpectedly comes home. We frantically throw our clothes on and switch off *Dancing Nancies* and pretend to watch video games. His mom walks into the center of the room and starts sniffing the air and finally says, utterly bewildered, "Why does it smell like tuna in here?"

Now that's too far back!

Perhaps back to college that night I was making out in the front seat of my car in a parking lot and another car pulled into the lot and its headlights illuminated our sexual encounter. My suitor looked at me. Startled. Scared. I followed his gaze and came to realize it wasn't the high beams flooding the car that had frightened him so, but the single, pubelike boob hair that stood on end like a defiant soldier.

No, just a little to the left of that.

I'm in Cancún and have been dancing with a towheaded guy named Steve, who seems to be the life of this south-of-the-border party. We stumble back to my hotel room and I go out on the balcony to yell and wave to my sorority sisters, who have passed out on lawn chairs poolside in order to secure chairs for morning. Steve and I begin making out, and without much warning, he pulls his pants and underwear off. Mind you, I still have my shoes on. He has a bit of trouble getting his khakis over his Tevas; I help him. He seems so focused. He then presents me with a mound of tangled, matted, disgruntled pubic hair. Beneath which is . . . a very large clitoris? A wine cork? A bottle cap? I shamelessly giggle but successfully play it off as though I am being coy. I attempt to clear the brush and get *at* it, but it—much like my hopes and dreams—is never to be reached. It's hard to excite something you can't see, but I somehow manage to get him excited, and a mushroom-capped nub emerges. A demented phoenix rises from a furball of ashes. I don't mean to be rude—surely I have a bit of extra flesh here and there—but to have so much less? And to have the audacity to display this stubby head to me with such fanfare is unforgivable. He starts thrusting his hips in the air, like when you do a bridge in yoga. His crotch is heaving up and down repeatedly, almost (dare I say) like we are having sex, but I am standing in front of the bed in a Billabong top and an Aéropostale skirt, my camera still hanging from my wrist should a cute pic present itself. It doesn't.

Now he is moaning. I realize this night is going to be . . . abstract. He can't have sex, so he is humping air and grunting like an animal. And it's musky from where I stand.

Maybe I imagine it, but I hear the sounds of laughter from down below as my friends giggle and gossip about the night. They are still children, I think. And here I have become a woman, being air-raped by a potato wedge. He is now clawing at the sides of the bed forcefully. Sensing he needs room, I take a step backward. He's gonna blow. Our eyes are locked in a horrifying stare. He is writhing up and down and the bed is thumping. He finally cries out. I wish I were there with you, dear reader, as you read this, so I could re-create it, but the best I can do is to say it sounded like, *"Ghhyytttndnnjnnfugygytyg!"*

Annnnnnnnd he comes on himself. His junglelike tufts are now gleaming and sticky. I feel sick. He smiles at me as if to say, "You're welcome."

I think that's enough for now. That walk down memory lane has taken its toll. What I would like to say is this: The woman whose words you have just read never learns and is always open to meeting anyone. Email me at Crossi3697@gmail.com. I'm not kidding.

HERE COMES THE LATE BLOOMER

by Katya Lidsky

I'm getting married this October. We've picked the menu and I found my dress and the guest list has been confirmed. I adore my fiancé—he is my best friend and such a good man and I could not ask for a more perfect partner. Everything is going along swimmingly, except for one thing: I didn't get to fuck enough.

I was a late bloomer. I was twenty-one when I lost my virginity. Yeah, that's right. Twenty-one. So late that my mom said, "Ay, Katica, thank God you finally did it. I thought you were a lesbian."

I missed out on four years of high school sex in the car and even prom-night boning. This is because I had no time for sex—I was too busy hating myself. I'm the middle daughter of three with a perfectionist streak, a tendency to be extreme about things, and a killer ability to be both self-punitive and rigid. . . the perfect recipe for a full-blown eating disorder! Yay! I mean, what's sexier than a girl who is so wildly insecure about her body she doesn't want anyone to touch her?! Does she count her calories for every meal? Oooooh . . . delicious. Does she work out with a crazed Charles Manson-esque look in her eye? Ahhhh . . . hot hot hot! Does she ram her arm down her throat and keep puking until she dry-heaves? I gotta get me some of that! You see, when french fries have the ability to send you into a tailspin of shame, it's kinda hard to be sexually free and learn about your body. The funny thing is that looking back, I think some guys did want to get a piece of this crazy. Realizing that now, I'm filled with regret. But more than that, I'm fucking furious.

I'm ticked off that I missed years and years of prime sexual freedom, sexual exploration, and sexual casualness. I don't mean being slutty; I was never the kind of girl who was gonna be a ho or be able to completely sever the emotional from the physical. But I could have had way more sex—I went to NYU! But I would never accept that someone was interested in me. Like that gorgeous guy who brought me Girl Scout cookies when I was sick and rubbed my feet. He didn't just want to be my friend. He probably wanted to put it in me! Or the guy who tipped me two hundred dollars for bringing him a vodka tonic when I worked as a cocktail waitress. It wasn't because it was the best vodka tonic he ever had. Maybe it was because I have big boobs and he wanted to snuggle his dick between them. The point is, I never thought guys saw me like that. I was the girl they talked *to* about other girls, not the one they talked about. I learned nothing about the power that comes from being a woman. I didn't get to delve into my femininity, and that makes me livid. Especially because I really like sex, but I just needed the safety of a serious relationship to feel comfortable enough to give my body away like that.

What a bummer.

And now that I'm coming into my own and actually *like* my body, now that I'm my most confident and even feel sexy sometimes, I get a ring on my finger. It's a really nice ring, but still. I wish this finger would have tickled a few more balls before it got ringed.

Here's another reason I'm pissed off. The only time I have ever slept with someone who wasn't a boyfriend, it was no fun. The *only* time! *One* time I got! And it was awful. Doesn't that seem entirely unfair to you? He was kinda like a one-night stand, except not really because I knew him. But for me it was risqué, so please just let me call it a one-night stand. It's all I've got.

I was in town visiting. He had seen me out. We exchanged numbers. Fast-forward: It's happening and he's taking off his boxers to display an entirely shaved lower region. Not one hair. Ten-year-old-boy style. Like he was trying to make it swim faster in a pool. The kissing was fine, he feels my boobs, blah blah blah—the truth is, I'm not really getting turned on. So does he tenderly kiss my neck or maybe use his tongue to excite my cherry blossom? Neither of those things, actually. He does his own trick. Not sure where he learned it, but it goes a little like this: He licks his hand, then smacks my nana as if it's a Heinz 57 bottle that he's trying to coax ketchup out of. He continues this dance, all the while looking at me as if to say, "I should be a porn star, huh?" Does he think he's gonna trick my vagina into thinking she's ready? Because my vagina is pretty smart. And she is not being fooled. She's as dry and unexcited as a vagina with slapped-on saliva can be. But committed to my one chance at a fling, I decide to go along with it and endure the chain of events.

Long story short, we had what I believe constitutes sex—although the friction from his hairless wiener and my unhydrated privates resulted in a sort of campfire smoke traveling upward from between my legs. It was hot . . . just not in the way I wanted it to be. I left aghast; I always thought these kinds of sexual escapades were supposed to be abnormally passionate, magically beautiful, and so intense and incredible that this bold flame could not endure . . . but must burn out with the sunrise. These are the musings of an ingenue who does not know better because she's never done this before. I definitely didn't deserve to get my hoo-ha slapped. And I certainly did not get even a taste of the carefree, exploratory, sexual freedom I craved. Where was an older man with the seasoned touch I had envisioned? Why not a foreigner whose travels and life I changed forever? How about a black man to rock my world and appreciate my Latin ass?

The next night at three in the morning I woke up to *boop-boop-beep-beep-baap*. A text message. "Come over and sit on my face," wrote the genital-shorn poet. I was horrified. Not about the come-and-sit-on-my-face part. I would have done that. It's the part about how he wanted me to come over there that pissed me off. Really? You want me to drive over there? Deal with finding parking? Walk around alone in the dead of night? How lazy can you be? At least if it's gonna be another night of lame vagina-slapping, make the effort. I'm not saying you have to climb the trellis to serenade me, but at least respect me enough to deal with parking near Runyon Canyon.

So I didn't get the rich sexual past I deserved. Instead I got crotch-spanked by a baldy. But I *do* get to marry the only man I've ever wanted to be family with, and I get to love him forever. I get to say "I do" and mean it. Besides, I have the rest of my life and a wonderful partner to catch up with. And he's not averse to dressing up like an Argentinian cattle farmer or a drifting cowboy, just to let me make up for lost time. I never have to have another experience that makes me want to barf. I've done enough barfing for one lifetime.

UNSENT LETTERS

by Matt McConkey

I've never been a one-night-stander. I'm more of a relationship guy, and no matter how many times I'm disappointed by one, I keep picking myself up, brushing myself off, and trudging into another one. I'm not always happy to embark on a new relationship. But here's a question: Is my dad happy to open his auto parts store every day at 7 a.m.? Hell, no. But he *shows up!* And that's the way I treat relationships. I don't always want to be there, but I'll be damned if I don't put in my time. Some call me a serial monogamist. Others call me a lesbian.

So yeah, I've been around the block a time or ten, and I suppose I've accumulated some bad-sex stories along the way. But let's be honest with ourselves: Does anyone really want to delve into the nitty-gritty of what happens when man-on-man sex goes awry? I don't. No, the piece I'd like to share with you is about penetrating a different hole—the one in my heart.

I decided to write an unsent letter to each of my former flames (my former flamers, if you will). And in lieu of a traditional bad-sex tale, I'm going to take this opportunity to finally, once and for all, *mail* these letters.

That's right. I'd like to mail them. I'd like to mail them from *my* heart . . . to *yours.*

Dear Marty,

I was intrigued every time I woke up to find you masturbating beside me, and then I was confused when you would get annoyed that I was there at all. But I still remember the good times, like getting stoned and baking cookies, and taking copious mental notes while you told me what I should change about my body.

Thanks for everything,
Matthew

Dear Jeremy from the Gym,

I enjoyed our time.

Our brief affair really made a lasting impression, like that time you slowly and carefully placed my hand on your six-pack as if it were a gift for me. (Thank you?) I believe that the moment you revealed your dream to be the next JC Chasez and started singing to me in bed (one of your original pop ballads, to boot) was the moment it was over (in my mind). And, okay, I have a confession to make: Sometimes, late at night, I find myself wondering: Did Jeremy from the Gym ever quit his human resources job to pursue his dream? And then I'll think, I want Pinkberry.

Fondly,
Lance Bass

Dear Andy from San Francisco,

You rocked my world.

You loved me, in spite of the fact that I had no car and lived in the kitchen. And I liked you, even though you never took your shirt off when it was, you know, naked time. (Not once.)

I want you to know that I forgive you for that time I drove all the way to visit you and you ditched me in a bar. Because I heard you gained a lot of weight since then. And I know you probably regret it.

Always,
Slim

Dear Ryan,

You're still on my mind. Yeah . . . even after all this time.

From late-night karaoke at Fubar to early-morning breakfast at IHOP, you sure know how to make a guy feel like a lady. And when you dropped the bomb on me over breakfast that you were already in a committed relationship, I thought to myself, Fuck! And then, when you added that your boyfriend was fourteen years old, my Rooty Tooty Fresh 'N Fruity almost came back up.*

Best,
Matty Boy

Yeah, you guys, I went out with a child molester. What? When he told me that, I almost flipped the table and performed a citizen's arrest on the motherfucker right then and there. But then I stopped. And I looked at him. And he was just so . . . into me, and I thought, Gosh . . . it's nice to feel young again. So I boned him anyway.

Okay, I didn't really bone him, but it makes for a snappier ending, don't you think? I don't really remember how it ended. I think I maybe finished my meal, and allowed him to pay for it, and said good-bye, and ignored his text messages. Snoresville, right? I mean, maybe he tried to smooch one more time at the end. And maybe I let him. But before you start pointing fingers, who among you can say you wouldn't do the same? You can't throw stones in child molesters' houses! Because they'd probably take those stones and rape them!

Dear Ollie,

We tried so hard. ("We." "You." Big whoop.)

I'll never forget the way your dirty talk sort of sounded like a middle-aged woman. And I'll never forget the day you said that you had *never heard of Amsterdam*. (Not "Where is Amsterdam?" but *"What* is Amsterdam?") But every time you described, in great detail, an episode of *Charmed*, I found it, well . . . charming.

I love that we still "check in" from time to time. Let's keep doing that. I always enjoy hearing that you're working as a day player on *That's So Raven* or doing background on *How I Met Your Mother*. I mean, yeah, it kinda seems like you're trying to make me jealous. But I think you're allowed to brag if you were the dumpee. So here's to your success.

Yours,

McConk (Your ex who was in a Super Bowl commercial in 2007. Remember that? That was awesome.)

Dear Noah,

You're five foot one.

I knew when I read your MySpace blog that was simply entitled "Life" that your journey from failed child actor to modeling agent was a very deep and meaningful one. And this isn't easy to say . . . but I wanted to tell you that when I saw you at La Poubelle with your new boyfriend, you looked . . . really happy.

And he sort of looked like . . . Judi Dench.

Sincerely,

Matt

Wow. That was quite a jaunt down memory lane, eh? Thanks for opening your hearts and taking that trip with me, everyone. This really got me thinking: It might be time for me to get back into the dating game. *Know what I mean, guys?* (I mean kill myself.)

xo,

mm

The End

Or is it . . . ?

A Sonnet

Scribed by Eric W. Pearson

Some men charge on when best they should retreat;
Thus find our man, woven betwixt the sheets;
Entwine'd with flesh etch'd by beauty and grace;
Body o'ershined, at least match'd by her face;
Fortune so great, pleasure he'd felt before;
Though prior sex had left his partner sore;
So on he thrusts, adjusts angles, and such.
Below our girl gets tense, for it's too much;
Alas, within her form discomfort grows;
And yet our man persists, he does not know;
Of pain that nags her delicate blossom;
A surge! Abrupt, with force that is awesome;
He reach'd climax as she appeal'd for peace;
And so, henceforth emerge'd: concerned release.

Glossary

A collection of terms you may have come across in this book or in your travels, newly introduced or existing and in need of definition

Ass Ninja
-noun
1. A mercenary agent (or ass-assin) highly skilled at the ancient art of anal play, best known for stealthy infiltration of the most guarded tunnels. The tactics of the ass ninja are in contrast to those of the "butt pirate," who, while pursuing the same end, lacks the discipline and subtle nature of the ninja.

Barebacking
-verb
1. Having sex without a condom.

Bear
-noun
1. A burly, lumberjack-like gay man, characterized by copious amounts of body hair, often bearded, and on occasion clad in plaid flannel.

BeHymen
-noun
1. The metaphorical seal of virginity of the anus, located behind the vagina and its hymen.

Black belt
-noun
1. The metaphorical reference to a sexual encounter with a black male or female, when the second party is not black. Also: white belt (Caucasian), brown belt (Latin), yellow belt (Asian), pink belt (homosexual), bible belt (religious), et cetera.

The Brown
-noun
1. The anus, or sphincter.

Butt-crack delta
-noun
1. The hollow at the top of the butt crack, where it meets the back; the nesting ground of the dick nugget.

Chickenheads
-noun
1. A gaggle of girls that stay together, look alike, and talk the same in incoherent high-pitched babble. They exist only as a unit and are easily startled.

The Cliterati
-noun
1. The elite academics of the female anatomy, learned in the art of its manipulation. The most cunning linguists.

See also: The Phallisophers

Comedy hot
-adjective
1. Used to describe the physically attractive qualities of a person in the comedy community, containing an implicit caveat that the same appreciation would not qualify under the standards of a larger population.

Dick nugget
-noun
1. A flaccid penis in its shrunken, post-coital state.

Diddle the skittle
-verb
1. Stimulation of the clitoris with the finger(s).

Douchebag
-noun
1. A person, typically male, possessed of offensive or revolting characteristics that may include, but are not limited to, sleaziness, lying, extreme cheesiness, narcissism, disproportionate affection for the band Linkin Park, an interrupting problem, incessant quotation of the movie *Old School*. Douchebags often possess the uncanny ability to bed a bevy of women, in spite of their douchebaggage.
–douche•bag•gage: tangible or intangible things (emotions, habits, loafers without socks) that identify the douche.

eHarm
-noun
1. The degradation, humiliation, disillusionment, and downgrading of standards and sense of self-worth that sometimes accompanies the use of online dating services.

Fauxgasm
-noun
1. The imitation of climax during intercourse while not actually experiencing orgasm.

Fingerblast
-noun
1. The rapid and repetitive movement of the finger(s) against the clitoris and/or vagina faster than any electronic device on the market.

Fuck buddy
-noun
1. A person one level below a "friend with benefits," as he/she is not truly a friend; a "buddy" or an "acquaintance" who is solely called upon to relieve sexual need derived from loneliness . . . and laziness.

Gaysian
-noun
1. A homosexual individual of Asian descent, and the innocent target of an easy pun.

Goat tits
-noun
1. Conical breasts that hang downward in a triangular rather than round silhouette, similar to the teats of a goat.

Gonzo's nose

-*noun*

1. A partially erect penis trapped in a downward-facing posture by underwear, resembling the nose of the character Gonzo from *The Muppets*.

Hermorrhage

-*noun*

1. A PMS-fueled temper tantrum, often followed by intense sobbing and complete emotional breakdown. Most commonly experienced by females, but can be non–gender specific.

Hummer

-*noun*

1. Euphemism for a blowjob, often accompanied by a voiced release of air for a pleasant vibrating sensation.

Ignoranus

-*noun*

1. One who has never experienced anal intercourse.

Moose knuckle

-*noun*

1. The asymmetrical double-bulge created by the penis and closest testicle when worn in snug-fitting trousers or underwear.
Synonym: Male camel-toe

Nano

-*noun*

1. A modern euphemism for the vagina, which, much like an iPod Nano®, can be made to produce

sound with a circular motion of the finger or thumb.

The Phallisophers

-*noun*

1. Those learned in phallisophy: the study of the male reproductive organ and its applications to life and all its questions, often possessed of a deep understanding of throat culture.
See also: The Cliterati

Porking

-*verb (to be porked)*

1. Grunty, squealing sex in an aggressive, repetitive motion. Pig-like intercourse.

Relationshit

-*noun*

1. Useless arguments, passive aggression, jealousy, and possessiveness, as well as mind games engaged by, upon, or between the parties of a romantic relationship.

Remember the Alamo!

-*exclamation*

1. Nostalgic reference to one's lost virginity.

Roasting

-*verb*

1. Something so degrading and disgusting we won't define it here. We do have *some* scruples. Google it if you must.

Shrimping

-*verb*

1. An act of foreplay involving taking a partner's toes into one's mouth and licking, sucking, or even chewing.

Skort

-noun

1. The apparel equivalent of a spork. Half skirt, half short. Originally developed to provide the modest gardener or bicyclist with both feminine style and coverage. Allows for physical activities ordinarily not advisable in a skirt, such as cartwheeling and dancing on bars. It is most commonly associated with the mid- to late-nineties.
2. A staple garment of the "cock-tease."
3. Acceptable on tennis courts ("sport the skort"). Unacceptable on Jessica Simpson.
4. "A mullet for your butt."

Social circle jerk

-noun

1. The group action of using its social circle as a sexual resource until all partner combinations and romantic options have been exhausted.
Synonym: Friendcest
2. An individual, or "jerk," who methodically sleeps his way through his social circle, at times crossing over into friends' social circles as well.

Sororitard

-noun

1. A female in a social environment exhibiting many of the characteristics of a stereotypical sorority girl; drunk, extroverted, and whoring for attention, consequently seeming somewhat retarded.

Strickly dickly

-adjective

1. Used to describe a person (man or woman) who categorically will engage sexually with a penis, not a vagina.

Tiny Town

-noun

1. The anus, when utilized for sexual penetration.

Twink

-noun

1. Young, fey homosexual male, generally attractive and delicate. Typically not eaten up with brains. Drawn to Beyoncé like a moth to flame. Gay jailbait.

Waist-up lesbian

-noun

1. A heterosexual female who enjoys homosexual activity involving the torso and face only.

Worst Laid Plan

-noun

1. An anecdote involving a plan to get laid, that turns out for the worst.
-verb

1. The act of planning to get "laid," only to have it take a turn for the worst.

CROSSWORD PUZZLE

Test your knowledge of the glossary terms.

Across

1 Piglike intercourse

4 The "other" sister

6 Funny-looking

7 Someone who's a little behind on the behind

11 A small village behind the big city

13 The mouth of the brown river

16 Friendcest

20 The pleasure of music

21 Memory of a battle lost

23 A climax . . . NOT!

24 Cock puppet

25 A digital explosion

Down

2 Beast breasts

3 A bad idea, made manifest

5 Fecal matters of the heart

8 Closet heterosexual female

9 To linger with fingers

10 Friend with benefits

12 Male camel-toe

14 Rhymes with "McNugget"

15 Emotional bloodletting

17 Gaggle of "birds," not geese

18 The gross guy's luggage

19 Taking off the safety

22 The metaphorical seal of the ass

Answer key on page 224

ABOUT THE EDITORS

Alexandra Lydon is originally from Boston, Massachusetts, and is a graduate of NYU's Tisch School of the Arts, where she earned a dual degree in drama and psychology. Alexandra created *Worst Laid Plans* with Laura Kindred after a tragically drunken evening in Galway, Ireland, and has played the role of coproducer, cowriter, and cast member since its conception. Alexandra is an actress currently living in Los Angeles. Some of her credits include the leading role in the independent film *Nail Polish*, television appearances on *Desperate Housewives*, *House*, *Private Practice*, *CSI*, *NCIS*, *Cold Case*, and recurring roles on *CSI: Miami*, *Prison Break*, and *24*.

* **Alexandra is attracted to emotionally unavailable, self-sabotaging, preferably alcoholic men, whom she thinks she can change.**

Laura Kindred was raised in Greater Boston, Massachusetts, and attended Phillips Academy Andover before earning a BFA from New York University's Tisch School of the Arts. Laura created *Worst Laid Plans* with accomplice Alexandra Lydon in the aftermath of poor decision-making abroad, and shares the mantle as producer and writer. Currently, Laura is a fashion and editorial writer in Los Angeles.

* **The first search result to appear if you Google Laura is *Butt Crack Bingo*.**

Photography by Alexis Cassar

ABOUT THE CONTRIBUTORS

*The following contributors are not victims, but by and large
the architects of their own misfortune. Because of that, a few have
chosen to remain pseudonymous. Others were more brave.*

Boti Bliss lives in Topanga and splits her time between starring on *CSI: Miami*, excessive self-obsessed soul-searching, and drinking too much wine.

Alison Brie is an actress and aspiring person of humor who lives in Los Angeles. She enjoys working on the award-winning drama series *Mad Men*, the hit comedy *Community*, and tripping the light fantastic.

Megan Brotherton was born and raised in Seattle, corrupted and demoralized in Los Angeles, and is currently being gentrified and aggrandized at Harvard University, where she is earning her MFA in acting.

Jackie Clarke is a writer and actor living in Los Angeles. Jackie has been sued by both her stepmother and *The Vagina Monologues* creator, Eve Ensler.

Whitney Cummings is a comedian who is regularly featured on *Chelsea Lately* and Comedy Central. When she's not feeling in control of her life she cuts her own bangs.

Dorien Davies is an actress, sketch writer, and puppeteer living in Los Angeles. She's a big fan of her husband, who has heard her story a bunch of times and apparently still finds her attractive.

Drew DiFonzo Marks is an improviser and actor living in Los Angeles. He performs and works regularly with the Upright Citizens Brigade Theatre. He usually has better sex than this, he swears.

Rachel F is a writer and a producer from New York City with terrible grammar. She remains anonymous due to a deep fear that her grandmother is going to read this book and find out she was a coke slut during the beginning of the twenty-first century.

Michael Feldman is a writer and performer living in Los Angeles with a New York heart. He tours the country with solo shows about religion, sexuality, body image issues, and, of course, awful sexual experiences.

John Flynn is a writer and performer who tells stories all over New York City. When he grows up, he wants to be Tim Gunn.

Nick Garfinkle is a successful Hollywood screenwriter; at least that's what his parents tell their friends.

Lindy Jamil Gomez is a regular on the UCB stage and cocreated and starred in the pilot *Out of Commission* with Laura Kindred. She is probably the only Hispanic and Lebanese half-breed to hail from Littleton, Colorado.

Tymberlee Hill (adoringly referred to by the men she dates as, "the loud, obnoxious, ape-limbed bitch in the corner") is an actor/writer working in Los Angeles. She specializes in making men better for the next girl they date.

Jennifer Hirshlag is a fashion and culture editor and writer who has worked for Style.com, *Women's Wear Daily*, Rizzoli, HarperCollins Publishers, and Penguin Group. She lives in Brooklyn, New York, with her husband, daughter, and canine bedmate, Zoey.

J. Janson got his start writing for sister Janise's underground feminist 'zine, *Once Upon A Ms*. Since moving to New York he is writing his own midnight shows and trying to follow the liberal life-path of his hero, Phil Donahue.

Laura Kindred (see editor bios)

Katya Lidsky is a dog trainer and founder of Shelter Shopper—a matchmaking service that brings people and shelter dogs together. She lives in Los Angeles with her lovely husband and doggies.

Beth Littleford you might know as one of the original correspondents on Comedy Central's *The Daily Show*. Or maybe from sitcoms, like ABC's *Spin City* or Fox's *Method & Red*. Or maybe as a spokesmodel for cheese. She's currently playing the mom of various teens on various shows and in various films. She's a mom in real life, too, which is even better.

Alexandra Lydon (see editor bios)

Wally Marzano-Lesnevich is a writer, actor, New York Mets fan, and social drinker, sometimes all at once. You may visit his Web site at worldofwally.com.

Matt McConkey can be seen in national commercials for cars, soda, beer, and burgers, or doing stand-up at the Comedy Store and the Improv. One time Jennifer Aniston bummed a cigarette from him.

Will McLaughlin is an actor and writer living in Los Angeles. He teaches improv at the Upright Citizens Brigade Theater. He apologizes to all he has wronged along the way.

Laraine Newman is a founding member of The Groundlings and an original cast member of *Saturday Night Live*. That has paved the way for her to do stupid voices for money, which she really likes and it sometimes gives her street cred. She has been married for twenty years and has two teenage daughters.

Michael J. Nice is a homosexual American and comic living in Los Angeles. He is a onetime contributor to *The Onion* and probably owes you money.

Eric W. Pearson reads so that he can write, and writes so that people will read.

Erin Pineda is an actress and writer who resides in Los Angeles. She is currently filming her mockumentary *The Heart Don't Know* and is thankful to the art of commercialism to keep her afloat. She is considering freezing her eggs. Special thanks to Josh Weinstein.

Mary Lynn Rajskub is a dramatic actress known for her role as computer genius Chloe O'Brien on the show *24*. She is also a stand-up comedian, which she became in 1994 after being laughed at during a performance art piece at the San Francisco Institute of Art.

June Diane Raphael is an actress and screenwriter living in Los Angeles. She cowrote *Bride Wars* with Casey Wilson and was recently seen opposite Jack Black and Michael Cera in *Year One*. She was named after June Cleaver from *Leave It to Beaver*.

Amy Rhodes lives in Los Angeles and currently writes for *The Ellen DeGeneres Show*. She's got great legs.

Zach Steel is a writer and actor. Credits include: this sentence and the sentence before this one.

"Suz" is a comedian who chooses to remain anonymous because she fears her mother will have a heart attack if she finds out she's gay.

Adria Tennor Blotta is an actress, writer, and expert pole dancer. She lives with her restaurateur husband, Claudio Blotta, in Los Angeles where the couple own and operate their wine bar and restaurant, barbrix, in Silver Lake.

Morgan Walsh is a regular writer and performer of sketch comedy at the Upright Citizens Brigade Theatre in Los Angeles. Credits include playing Peter Dinklage's tattooed lover in *Surviving Eden* and roles such as "Almost Flashing Girl" in the FX show *It's Always Sunny in Philadelphia*.

Casey Wilson was a featured player on *Saturday Night Live,* and her film credits include *For Your Consideration* and *Julie and Julia*. She regularly performs at the Upright Citizens Brigade Theatre. Along with June Raphael, she cowrote the film *Bride Wars*.

A SPECIAL THANKS AND SPANKS TO: The Upright Citizens Brigade Theatre, Jenny Bent, Neil Campbell, David Cashion, Alexis Cassar, The Cassars' backyard, Tymberlee Hill, Drew DiFonzo Marks, Janeane Garofalo, Reyna Godoy, David Harris, Jennifer Hirshlag, Jimmy Jatho, Jessica Julius, Natalie Kindred, Anthony King, Gabrielle Krengel, Matt McConkey, Bob McGowan, Laraine Newman, Eric Pearson, Erin Pineda, Amy Poehler, June Diane Raphael, Mary Lynn Rajskub, Sarah Self, Jonathan Shikora, Aaron Stanford, Jake Weiner and everyone at Benderspink, and Casey Rose Wilson.

And to all our audience for coming again and again. We didn't.

CROSSWORD ANSWER KEY

Across		Down	
1	Porking	2	Goat Tits
4	Sororitard	3	Worst Laid Plan
6	Comedy Hot	5	Relationshit
7	Ignoranus	8	Waist Up Lesbian
11	Tiny Town	9	Diddle the Skittle
13	Butt Crack Delta	10	Fuck Buddy
16	Social Circle Jerk	12	Mooseknuckle
20	Hummer	14	Dick Nugget
21	Remember the Alamo	15	Hermorrhage
23	Fauxgasm	17	Chickenheads
24	Gonzo's Nose	18	Douchebaggage
25	Fingerblast	19	Barebacking
		22	Behymen

The End

Seriously.

For now . . .